It's Your Money . . .
It's Your Future . . .
Don't Blow It!

*How to manage
your money with
ease and confidence*

Greg Hicks
Wanda Cooper

Liberty Publishing Group

Cover Design: Cher Holton

Publisher's Cataloging-in-Publication Data

Hicks, Greg .
    It's Your Money ... It's Your Future ... Don't Blow It!
: How to manage your money with ease and confidence /
Greg Hicks and Wanda Cooper.
    p. cm.

    ISBN 1-893095-40-1

Library of Congress Control Number: 2005922565

10 9 8 7 6 5 4 3 2 1

Acknowledgements

To my great staff team who has faithfully blessed my business over the last few years with their talent, commitment and loyalty, allowing us all to prosper in every way; Leanne Chamblee, Jenni McInnes, Susan MacDonald, Emily Renfrow, Karen Bullock and Carla Towns.

~ Greg Hicks

To my Lord and Savior, who gave me strength and provided wisdom when I needed it. I will always be grateful for the years I spent in the banking world where I learned so much. A special thank you to my husband, Rick, who always believes in me, and to my children, Richard and Jordan, who didn't mind the time I spent writing this book. And last, but certainly not least, I will always be grateful for my clients in both our personal and business relationships.

~ Wanda Cooper

TABLE OF CONTENTS

*"Obstacles are things a person sees when
he takes his eyes off the goal."*
Joseph Crossman

Introduction

George Bernard Shaw once quipped, "The lack of money is the root of all evil." There is some truth to his words. We often ask people in our seminars, "How many of you have a problem that a little money would solve right now?" Lots of hands go up into the air.

We have spoken to and counseled hundreds of people in person and thousands of people in meetings, seminars and on our radio shows. One clear picture emerges before us —people really do not understand money and wealth. Americans are more adept at making money than using it wisely to reach their personal goals.

Money, like other certain items in life, is essential. The use or misuse of money can provide you freedom or make you a slave, become a positive influence or destroy your life. The amount of money is far less important than the wise use of the money.

Lack of knowledge can be a dangerous thing, and being deceived can be even more dangerous. As financial advisors, we spend much of our time educating people in the wise use of assets and income. Increasingly however, we find ourselves trying to undo or repair the results of a poor financial decision that was initiated from the bad advice from a bad advisor. The word "bad" means everything from ignorant to incompetent and from self-serving to ripping people off. Suffice it to say that there is much misrepresentation and misinformation among financial advisors.

The purpose of this book is to be a guide in wisdom regarding financial matters. It is written in simple short chapters covering fifteen different topics—all important for you to know. We filled it with true stories of real people (names, dates and circumstances changed to provide confidentiality). This book is extremely practical and is modeled after our weekly radio shows and periodic seminars. We purposely mean to make the complicated become simple.

Everyone has a financial plan—most people have a poor one. Our goal is not to make you rich but to make you rich in the wisdom of handling money and assets.

Financial planning is complicated and ever changing. We believe wise counsel will provide a path for you to see your rewards and reach your goals. It is never too late to begin the journey towards financial and personal wellbeing. We hope this book will become a valuable resource for you as you grow in financial wisdom.

"The naïve believes everything, but the prudent man considers his steps ... without consultation plans are frustrated, but with many counselors they succeed."
King Soloman (Proverbs 14:15 & 15:22)

"Not admitting a mistake is a bigger mistake."
Robert Haef

Chapter 1

The Most Common Financial Mistakes People Make

1 **Making financial decisions with unreliable, inaccurate, and misinformation**

Most people base many of their decisions on trust. Because of this I am not surprised when I meet with people who come to me for a review and I find they have been "sold a bill of goods." The job of a financial planner is to identify the goals of the person and to use investment products that help them accomplish their goals.

For example, there are numerous people, especially seniors I have met who were "sold" annuities and life insurance as a tool to meet their goals. There is absolutely nothing wrong with life insurance and annuities except in some cases these people already owned annuities and did not need to "switch" to another product.

One particular case involved a woman who owned an annuity with a well known insurance company and her goal for this annuity was to leave it to her five grandchildren. An insurance agent convinced her that the best way to accomplish this was to exchange this one annuity for five different annuities (the only thing she actually needed to do was to list the five grandchildren as beneficiaries). This recommendation only created commission for the agent and because annuities have a surrender period, these five new annuities all had five new surrender periods. Her old annuity's surrender period was over at the time of the switch. She already had a perfectly good investment and change was not necessary, however, she was misinformed and mislead. The only "winner" in this exercise was the agent who pocketed a nice commission.

I have also met with "wealthy" individuals who were "sold" life insurance policies to cover estate taxes when the estate was not large enough for estate taxes to be a concern. The agent convinced the so-called "wealthy" person that her investments would increase in value so much that her heirs would owe estate taxes at her death. This agent never once mentioned the Economic Growth and Tax Relief Act of 2001 which states that beginning in 2002, the Federal estate tax exemption would be $1 million and in 2004 would increase to $1.5 million, etc. She paid over $100,000 in premiums over 8 years for a policy she did not need.

Another area where seniors especially lack correct information is that of Medicaid planning. This is a dilemma for the senior because to qualify for Medicaid long-term care, the senior has to be at "poverty" level (below $2000 in assets in NC). Being aware of these criteria, seniors often times transfer their assets to children. This could be a problem for the senior in that they lose control and could potentially lose their assets. In the situation where assets are transferred to children, seniors run the risk of potentially losing their home or their liquid assets due to the adult child's credit problems or a divorce. If this is not a concern then do remember that the "disqualifying waiting period" for Medicaid is 36 months and in the case of transfers to trust, the waiting period is 5 years. This means that if a senior applied for Medicaid before the three or five year waiting period, the gifted assets would disqualify them. Seek help from a professional such as an attorney or a certified financial planner prior to a transfer of assets.

In addition, the children inherit a problem, because when a parent gifts highly appreciated assets such as land, their home or old stocks, the children "inherit" the original cost basis. So when they sell the assets, there will be a potentially severe capital gains tax liability. This brings us to the next big mistake.

2 Failure to own property correctly

There are basically four ways to own property:
- ➢ Own it yourself
- ➢ Own it jointly with a spouse
- ➢ Own it with someone other than your spouse
- ➢ Own it inside of a trust with you as a potential trustee

Let's examine each of the four ways...

Owning property yourself

You have total control of the asset. It's yours, you own it, all tax issues are yours.

Owning property jointly with a spouse

Is this a good idea? Usually it is a good idea, however, it could supercede the wishes of your will. How? What if your will says you want to leave your $50,000 CD to Sue and your $150,000 home on the river to John, but each of those assets are owned jointly with your spouse. Who gets them? Your spouse, that's who.

Joint ownership takes precedence over wills and trusts. You must coordinate your ownership of assets with your will or trust documents, or there could be some monumental mess-ups.

Joint with someone other than your spouse

What about owning property with someone *other* than your spouse? The main problem with this is property held jointly is subject to the claims of creditors or lawsuits. For example, for safety reasons you add your daughter's name to your bank CD just in case something happens to you. Now she owns half of the CD. Then suddenly her husband files for bankruptcy. Your CD may be subject to claims from his creditors and you could end up losing the whole bank CD to the creditor (if your goal was to do Medicaid or estate planning, there are other options such as trust or wills).

Ownership by trust
(see chapter on Estate Planning)

Living trusts, revocable trusts and irrevocable living trusts all allow you to avoid probate. All trusts provide a level of confidentiality as well.

Revocable Trust (Living Trust): This trust is excellent for probate avoidance and confidentiality, but does not provide tax avoidance (neither income tax nor estate tax). Assets are held in the name of the trust with you or you and your spouse or child as trustees.

Credit Shelter Trust (By Pass Trust): This trust is designed for couples only and does provide estate tax shelter capacity up to the level that current Federal tax law allows. It allows you to pass many more assets to your children, while avoiding estate taxes.

Irrevocable Living Trust: This trust is set up to remove assets from your estate to avoid estate taxes. It is used only by high net worth people. Once the assets are removed, they are out of your control in most cases.

Special Needs Trust: This trust is designed for beneficiaries who have a special medical, mental or physical problem and cannot care for themselves properly. A trustee handles the trust assets and income for the benefit of the beneficiary.

All of these trusts allow you to change the title of your assets. It is an entity that holds your assets. You can create the terms of the trust to suit you and have your assets distributed in the manner that you wish. Always seek professional advice when setting up a trust.

3 Protecting assets from unforeseen risks

What are the risks to your assets?

Market risk—many of you reading this have heard the analogy, "The higher the risk the higher the return, lower risk, lower return." Some risk for a potential better return is needed especially for "longer term money" or money needed in the distant future. Assets that you may be deriving income from today should not be in the higher "risk" category. If you are under 50 years of age and are looking for growth, clearly some risk is wise to reach longer term goals.

After retirement, the investment portfolio goal is typically structured to provide the retiree with growth and income along with reasonable preservation of principal and tax advantages. Seniors who are inclined to lean toward highly conservative investments that focus entirely on safety of principal often find their portfolios eroded by inflation risk. Inflation historically decreases the buying power of money over time, so seniors should consider incorporating at least a small portion of growth-oriented investments such as stock. The following chart is helpful.

Overcoming Taxes and Inflation

$10,000 Twelve month CD @ 4.5%	= $450.00
Minus taxes (33% tax bracket)	= -$150.00
	$300.00
Minus inflation (3% average)	= -$300.00
Real Return	**= $0**

8

Inflation causes the dollar to lose purchasing power over time.

Diversification risk—remember the old saying, "Don't put all your eggs into one basket?" This holds true in your financial plan as well. No one should subject all his or her money to just one investment. So how do you take risk properly? It is done through asset allocation.

The Rewards of Diversification
How to Potentially Decrease Risk While Increasing Returns

Year	Large-Co Stocks	Small-Co Stocks	Real Estate Stocks	Foreign Stocks	U.S. Bonds
1984	6.27	-7.30	**20.93**	7.38	15.15
1985	31.73	31.05	19.10	**56.16**	22.10
1986	18.66	5.68	19.16	**69.44**	15.26
1987	5.25	-8.80	-3.64	**24.63**	2.76
1988	16.56	25.02	13.49	**28.27**	7.89
1989	**31.63**	16.26	8.84	10.54	14.53
1990	-3.11	-19.48	-15.35	-23.45	**8.96**
1991	30.40	**46.04**	35.70	12.13	16.00
1992	7.61	**18.41**	14.59	-12.17	7.40
1993	10.06	18.88	19.65	**32.56**	9.75
1994	1.31	-1.82	3.17	**7.78**	-2.92
1995	**37.53**	28.45	15.27	11.21	18.47
1996	22.95	16.50	**35.27**	6.05	3.63
1997	**33.35**	22.36	20.26	1.78	9.65
1998	**28.60**	-2.55	-17.50	20.00	8.69
1999	21.03	21.26	-4.62	**26.96**	-0.82
2000	-9.10	-3.02	**26.37**	-14.17	11.63
2001	-11.88	2.49	**13.93**	-21.44	8.44
2002	-22.09	-20.48	3.82	-15.94	**10.25**
2003	28.67	**47.25**	37.13	38.59	4.10

*Average annual total returns for each sector are from 1984-2003. The bolded results indicate the best performer for the year.
Sources: Lipper Inc., National Association of Real Estate Investment Trusts

All of us face the financial challenge of ensuring that not only our assets grow, but that our resources last. Under most circumstances an allocation of an individual's portfolio into stocks is considered the appropriate long-term means to address inflation both before and during retirement, however, because the stock market is volatile, this strategy could be uncomfortable for many people. Diversification is a recognized strategy for reducing risk and improving overall portfolio performance. Although diversification does not guarantee positive returns or preservation of principal, it does offer a measure of protection against market fluctuation. In review of a person's portfolio, an advisor should consider the level of diversification among various asset classes such as stocks, bonds, real estate, mutual funds and cash. Even within the stock assets, allocation should be made among, fast growing, more stable slow growing companies, domestic, international, large, medium and small companies.

An investment portfolio should provide the person with growth and income along with reasonable preservation of principal plus tax advantages. The asset mix is periodically adjusted to market changes and to the age of the client.

The investment world is always changing and improving. For example, there are now even mutual funds that offer principal protection. This is attractive for those investors that desire to participate in the market, but do not want the fear of potentially losing any of their principal. Of course there is a cost to receiving this kind of guarantee. Typically mutual funds have an estimated annual expense ratio of 0.5-2.5%, yet a fund that offers a principal guarantee could potentially have a higher expense ratio. Also, there is usually a time commitment of at least five years. All guarantees cost something. Even a bank CD has its cost. The bank offers to you a guarantee of principal and interest on your CD as long as you leave the CD for the agreed term. Should you liquidate the CD before the "maturity date," you could potentially lose a portion of your earned interest. Guarantees can cost time and money, but having a peace of mind about your money is priceless.

Before I leave this subject, allow me to mention briefly that annuities also offer a guaranteed living benefit. For example, there are several good variable annuity companies that guarantee you will receive a 5% guaranteed return on your principal for every year you own the annuity no matter how the market performs. There is also a higher expense ratio to receive this benefit. Remember the surrender charge on any annuity can vary from 0 to 9 years.

A well-diversified financial plan involves the coordination of multiple financial elements and careful consideration of different life stages of a person. A good financial plan, properly allocated, can offer you peace of mind, security and a sense of control.

4 Failure to match goals with the correct financial instrument

The majority of long-term investment instruments held by most investors are real estate, stocks, bonds, mutual funds and annuities. What combination is right for you?

In working with people, an advisor must gather the data, analyze it, develop a plan, implement and monitor the plan along the way. Gathering and analyzing data helps the advisor match your goals with the appropriate financial instruments. You must be willing to share with your advisor your goals and your feelings about risks, as well.

Your portfolio could be summed up as two categories: short term and long-term. Long-term is usually 5 or more years. Short term investments also have a place in your portfolio. CD's, savings accounts, money markets and checking accounts are examples of short term investment tools. These are good for emergency money and paying bills. A general rule of thumb is 3 to 6 months of expenses should be maintained in a cash accessible short term instrument. I have seen cases where long-term investments remained in a short term investment vehicle. By doing this, you lose purchasing power. Put simply; you will be able to buy less food tomorrow than you can today, as inflation has its way on a low returning investment.

I also recommend that people who need income from their investments divide their portfolio in two ways: investments that generate income and investments that have long-term growth potential. Again it is important to communicate with your advisor the goals you have for your money.

There is a common error made because of not adjusting your investment products as you age. For example, from time to time I meet seniors who continue to make premium payments on life insurance that either is not needed or there is enough cash value to cover the entire death benefit. We have seen policies with a $50,000 death benefit with $46,000 of cash value. So what is the risk to the insurance company? (The insurance company loves you!)

If your answer is $4,000, you are correct. In this case, I would have to say that it might be better to move that cash value to an investment instrument that generates income, such as an annuity, or call the company and get a "paid up" policy with a higher death benefit and no more premiums.

Go with your instincts! If the investment tool recommended to you just doesn't seem a fit, don't do it. If you have not re-evaluated your investments later and adjusted the choices to your current goals, call a good advisor today.

5 Failure to Reduce Taxes, Fees and Commissions

Wherever possible, avoid, reduce or postpone taxes. Keep more of your hard earned money. For example, if you have investments that create taxable returns or interest, consider moving them to tax deferred or tax free investments. Millions of people invest in mutual funds and every year at tax time they get a 1099. You could avoid this by owning mutual funds under a variable annuity or owning tax efficient funds. Of course liquidating the mutual funds to accomplish this change could create a taxable event, but sometimes it may not. If you have owned these mutual funds for a number of years then you have paid capital gains all along so it may be possible to liquidate then and not incur taxes. Call your mutual fund company to find out where you stand.

Giving can reduce taxes. You can gift to your favorite charity highly appreciated stocks, mutual funds and bonds. Consider this in lieu of cash. Remember when you sell a stock you pay capital gains, but the charity does not and everyone wins except the IRS.

Here's a stock gifting example:

Purchase 100 shares @ $10/share = $1,000
Current Value @ $25/share = $2,500
Capital Gain of $15/share = $1,500

SELLING	GIVING
$1,500 Gain x 22% Tax Bracket (Capital Gains) *$ 330 Taxes Due*	$2,500 Gift x 30% Tax Bracket (Income) *$ 750 Taxes Saved*

Giving stocks in lieu of cash increases your cash flow as well because as you are giving your stock you are not writing checks from your checkbook.

What if you are one of the "lucky" ones to have owned stocks during 2001 and 2002? You probably experienced considerable loss (on paper if you chose not to sell). You can sell that stock, take the loss and repurchase that same stock 31 days later. This is referred to as a wash sale. It is perfectly legal to do so—claim the write off and tax deductions, then own the stock again as it hopefully goes back up.

Another good way to reduce taxes and increase your income stream is through a tool known as the Charitable Remainder Trust (CRT). With the CRT you can lower your current income taxes, avoid capital gains and maintain or even increase your income for life. (See chapter on Protecting Your Estate for details concerning the CRT)

One way to save taxes on distribution of retirement money is something called a "stretch IRA." A "stretch IRA" gives you the ability to stretch your IRA over the lifetime of your children or other beneficiaries and in essence become part of their retirement. They simply receive the minimum distribution annually, based on their age, but since they are younger the minimum distribution is significantly less, so the remaining assets grow for years more, tax deferred. What a benefit to them! Your IRA becomes an income generating asset for your beneficiaries. To accomplish this, all of your beneficiaries have to be listed as primary beneficiaries or contingent beneficiaries before you die. Beneficiaries cannot be added after your death. This concept can even be applied to annuities as well.

6 Health Care: Not Planning for long-term care, disability, Medicare and Medicaid

What is long-term care and what are your options should you or your loved one need long-term care?

Long-term care, also referred to as extended care, is a catch all phrase that describes three levels of care: skilled care, home care and custodial care. Let's take some time to understand each level of care.

Skilled Care: This is care provided under a doctor's order by a licensed professional such as a nurse or physical therapist in a nursing home or skilled care facility.

Home Care: This is care provided in your home by a home healthcare nurse.

Custodial Care: This is care that is most often needed for the longest period of time. This level of care provides assistance with activities of daily living such as bathing, dressing, toileting and eating.

What is the cost of long-term care?

According to Metlife's Mature Market Institute, the average cost of nursing home care is $153.00 per day. Of course this can vary depending on your region. Remember the facility is only part of the cost. There are additional charges for prescriptions, dentures, eyeglasses or personal needs.

Home health care may be quite costly depending on the amount of outsider help coming into the home. This cost can range from $12.00 to $24.00 per hour.

Options that many people believe pay for long-term care are: Medicare, Medicaid supplements and long-term care policies. In reality, the two largest payers of long-term care are patient out-of-pocket (39%) and Medicaid (31%). Medicare pays up to 100 days per benefit period, but with strings attached.

> ➢ Days 1-20 Medicare pays 100%
> ➢ Days 21-100 Medicare pays all but a daily coinsurance amount
> ➢ After 100 days, no coverage unless read-mitted to hospital first

For Medicare to pay, the facility must be a Medicare approved facility. Medicare will pay 100% of all covered and medically necessary home health services.

On the other hand, Medicaid is a jointly funded venture between federal and state governments. It is first and foremost, a welfare program with stringent financial eligibility requirements. It provides a critical safety net for those who cannot pay for long-term care. Those facilities relying primarily on Medicaid funding cannot match the quality of care that is received at private pay facilities. More importantly, not all nursing homes take Medicaid patients and beds are not always available in the desired location. Patients who are admitted as private pay patients and later convert to Medicaid may have to move if the facility does not take Medicaid. In most states, Medicaid does not typically cover home care either. The changing nature of the Medicaid program makes it an uncertain planning option at best.

long-term care insurance policies have evolved from nursing home only policies to comprehensive policies that cover nursing home, assisted living, home health care and adult day care. Selecting a policy requires making some important decisions. The choices you must make include:

> ➤ How much will the daily dollar amount be?
> ➤ Should inflation protection be included?
> ➤ How long will the benefit period be?
> ➤ How long will the elimination period be? (before the benefit income begins)
> ➤ What type of care will be provided? (i.e.; nursing home, home health care or adult day care)

There are now policies that will allow you to combine a life insurance policy with long-term care benefits. This eliminates the fear of paying premiums into long-term care and never using it. Figure 1.1 provides an example.

Tax Benefits of Life/Long-Term Care Insurance

> ➤ Tax-Deferred Growth
> ➤ Long-Term Care Benefits Paid Income Tax-Free
> ➤ Unused LTC Benefits Pass Income Tax-Free Benefits to Heirs

> *We do not provide specific tax advice.*
> *Check with your personal tax advisor.*

The current system for financing long-term care costs is bankrupting families and burdening taxpayers. Congress and the administration are debating reduced government funding for Medicare and Medicaid. The decision to purchase or not

Is Self-Insuring Long-Term Care a Good Solution?

Male Age 69
Female Age 59
Joint Age 62   **LIFE INSURANCE WITH**
Non-smoker in goodhealth   **LONG-TERM CARE**

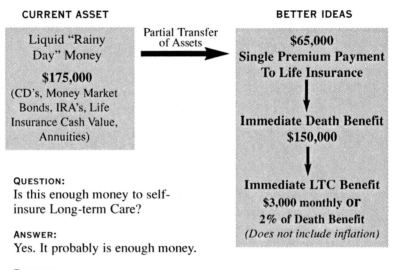

CURRENT ASSET

Liquid "Rainy Day" Money

$175,000
(CD's, Money Market Bonds, IRA's, Life Insurance Cash Value, Annuities)

Partial Transfer of Assets →

BETTER IDEAS

$65,000
Single Premium Payment To Life Insurance
↓
Immediate Death Benefit $150,000
↓
Immediate LTC Benefit
$3,000 monthly or
2% of Death Benefit
(Does not include inflation)

QUESTION:
Is this enough money to self-insure Long-term Care?

ANSWER:
Yes. It probably is enough money.

EXAMPLE
$120/day for care x 1,460 Days (4 years) = $175,200

PROBLEM:
The only way for this "plan" to work is to leave the entire $175,000 alone.

*Premium could be paid by single premium or over a 10-year period.

Figure 1.1 Is Self-Insuring Long-Term Care a Good Solution?

purchase long-term care insurance may affect the entire family for many years to come.

Perhaps a more immediate issue for people age 20-60 is disability insurance. Think of it as income replacement. People between the ages of 20-60 are much more likely to be disabled than to die. Here is a realistic question to ask yourself, "How long could my family last without income?"

Usually the answer is, "Not too long!" Be sure to take a long hard look at our chapter on Insurance to assess your risk and your income needs.

All the planning and investing in the world could come crashing down if a person does not plan for a potential catastrophic event. None of us are immune. Hopefully by revealing these potential mistakes that are so common to all of us, you can take immediate steps to insure your financial future.

7 Procrastination

The biggest problem in financial planning is not lack of money; it is procrastination. Human nature dictates that we tend to be bound up in what seems urgent rather than what is really important. Even more, we program ourselves from an early age to make decisions and perform activities based upon a deadline. When the class paper comes due, we are working late into the night to finish the product. Deadlines produce results! Whether the results are quality or slipshod is another question.

To a 25-year-old, retirement seems a hundred years away. Need insurance? No, frankly a 25-year-old is pretty sure they are indestructible. At that age, making a mistake is no problem because there is so much time to fix it. Then the marriage and the kids come along. Life becomes a whirlwind of activity. One day, before you know it, the kids are finishing college, getting married and you are 55 years old! Do you have a will? Did you invest wisely? Did you save on taxes? Did you buy the wrong house, with the wrong mortgage? Did you wait too long to max out your 401(k) or insure your risks? Or did you put off some

19

important things? No problem, maybe the government will take care of it for me. Yeah, right!

Procrastination in financial planning almost never works to your benefit and usually costs you the money or time—two things you really need lots of during the ages of 60-90. Oh well, maybe working at age 75 is not so bad after all, while living with your kids in their spare bedroom!

Don't delay, do it today! Never put off an important financial planning decision. You will pay a price for sure—one day. This book will nail down many action points that you will need to consider. Read on, take notes, and activate your financial plans now!

Notes

"Money is to be respected; one of the worst things you can do is handle another person's money without respect for how hard it was to earn."
(T. Boone Pickens, Jr.)

"We cannot direct the wind but we can adjust the sails."
Author unknown

Chapter 2

Choosing a Financial Advisor & How to Avoid a Bad Advisor

The question is not, "Do I need financial planning advice?" The question is, "What kind of advice did I get?" How does one go about finding a good quality financial advisor with integrity? Friends and family are a good first referral source. You may even begin with the local chamber of commerce and interview financial advisors that are members, although this is no guarantee. Accountants and lawyers could also be good referral sources, but be careful. Even before you begin your search, you may want to ask yourself, "What do I want a financial planner or advisor to do?" Do you want to just buy stocks or bonds or do you want a professional who can create a comprehensive financial plan and help you by coordinating the efforts of other professionals in putting your plan into action?

The norm today is that everyone who is somehow involved in banking, investing or insurance, claims to be a financial planner or advisor. Nothing could be further from the truth! Just because a profession revolves around money does not qualify a person to be called a financial advisor. For example, a bank branch manager licensed to sell mutual funds is not a qualified financial advisor, other than maybe for mutual funds. Another example would be the insurance salesman giving advice on investments or estate planning and only using life insurance or annuities as a way of meeting your objectives. Both these examples could lead to bad news for you (with losses) and good news for the advisor (with commissions).

Quality financial planners look at all assets including real estate, life insurance, cash, retirement plans, etc. Your debts, expenses and income are also a consideration, as well as tax savings. A good financial planner will ask you about your current goals as well as your future goals and your reason for seeking a financial planner. In your meeting with a financial planner, you should do most of the talking and the planner should do most of the listening.

You Have to Trust Someone!

A list of credentials you may want to look for in an advisor are:

> **Education:** Don't be overly concerned if their college degree is in something other than accounting or finance as long as their training is in financial planning and their licenses are in the financial disciplines that you need.

> **State or Federal Registration & Licensing:** Many states require that planners be registered and pass exams. Insurance and

securities licenses are needed in every state. Your state securities office can tell you if a financial professional is licensed to charge a fee for managing securities. Websites include *www.nasdr.com* and *www.sec.gov.* Also check for complaints with your local Better Business Bureau.

The means in which a planner is compensated is important. All planners are compensated in one of three ways:

1. **Fee Based:** Planners who charge by the hour ($75.00 - $250.00) or a flat annual fee ($1,000.00 - $5,000.00) or as a percentage of managed assets (1-3% annually).

2. **Commission:** Planners who are commission based are paid by the products they recommend. All investments and insurance products have some form of transaction fees, expenses or sales charges. The planner is paid from the fees or commissions within the mutual fund, insurance product, stock trade or bond trade.

3. **Fee Plus Commission:** This would mean that the planner makes a commission on the investment and collects a fee for providing the financial plan.

So with all that said, "Which way is best?" I will have to answer that with, "It depends."

A good planner will be worth the money because they can help make the process of wealth accumulation fun and profitable for you, and save you time, taxes and money.

Integrity Does Matter!

Your comfort level with the advisor is the most important item. Fees and commissions are not the most important item, contrary to popular opinion. The advisors character and integrity are paramount. Trust is the vital ingredient to a successful relationship. Let's be honest – you will have to trust someone. This is unavoidable and must be dealt with right up front as you begin your client-advisor relationship. Once you choose the planner or advisor, develop the relationship. Remember if you are in a client-advisor relationship that is not comfortable, you can always move to a better situation.

Key Question: Are there bad advisors? And are there bad advisors who give bad advice? Yes and yes!

Time and space will not allow us to share all of our experience with clients who have received bad advice. But we will share a few horror stories with you to make the point.

Life Insurance Advisors

Senior citizens seem to be a target of unethical insurance salesmen/advisors. For example, one 75-year-old woman was convinced by an insurance agent to purchase a $200,000 universal life insurance policy with a premium price tag of $14,000 per year. The pretense for the recommendation was that her current stock portfolio would grow so fast that she would surely owe estate taxes at her death. There was only one problem, no, two problems. One, she was exempt from Federal estate taxes because her portfolio value was too small and two, her estate values were estimated to keep growing at over 20% annually. Clearly this was horrible advice. By the time we met with her she had paid several annual premiums. Wasted money, wasted time, wrong advice! And the agent made lots of money!

Another scheme that we often see is insurance policies which build cash value are being sold as retirement plans. Since the cash value inside of some policies grows tax deferred and can be withdrawn under certain conditions tax free, it can be made to look like a retirement plan. However, the first question should always be, "Do I need life insurance and if I do, how much?" The second question should be, "Have I taken advantage of all other retirement strategies such as 401K, 403(b), Traditional IRA, Roth IRA, etc?" Only then should you proceed with any advisor who is selling life insurance as a way to accumulate retirement assets. Several companies have been sued for selling insurance as retirement plans.

IRA's and Rollovers

All IRA vehicles have tax issues that must be addressed. Bad advisors conveniently forget to alert naïve investors sometimes regarding the tax issues. For example, one client over 70 years old was pressured at an estate planning seminar and a subsequent personal appointment to convert his large Traditional IRA to a Roth IRA so his heirs would be able to save taxes one day. The advisor conveniently left out one rather large tax issue. The client would have to pay income taxes now, in the year of the conversion to the tune of tens of thousands of dollars. Can you imagine the surprise next year when the tax bill came due? Fortunately we intercepted the transfer request before the conversion took place. We discussed the problem and the lucky client stopped the transfer in it tracks.

Churning Accounts

Every investment account could be a target for an unethical investment advisor who is on the prowl for extra commissions. For example, some unsuspecting investors sign a limited power of attorney form which allows an investment representative to place trades in their account without calling the investor. Commissions are generated upon each trade. We have seen clients whose statement revealed the advisor purchasing the same stock over and over a few days apart or selling and buying the same stock a few days apart. Think about the client's statement each month. If the investor did not look closely at the account activity section, they would not have noticed that the stock last month was still there this month. The unsuspecting investor was nailed with two commissions – selling and buying and was unaware this happened.

In later chapters in this book more examples of bad advice are highlighted. Pay attention and keep alert to the unscrupulous men and women who disguise themselves as financial advisors.

Notes

"I love to go to Washington -- if only
to be near my money."
(Bob Hope)

*"A family budget is a process of checks and balances—
the checks wipe out the balances."*
Arthur Langer

Chapter 3

It's Not What You Earn, It's What You Keep

One of the more mundane, yet necessary areas of financial planning is the area of cash flow and budgeting. Certainly this subject does not arouse excitement like purchasing a stock or a piece of real estate. Yet cash flow is the most repetitive and common issue facing every person. If one doesn't budget properly there will be an immediate repercussion. On the other hand, having a proper budget and cash flow can bring immense freedom and can easily lead to reaching both short term and long term goals.

In the financial planning business we rarely meet with anyone who has great budgeting skills. What drives people to seek financial advice is improper budgeting, a loss of income or an increase of expenses. Sometimes a traumatic event can trigger the necessity of a meeting for counseling. A job loss, an injury or an accident can create havoc in one's budget or cash flow. On the positive side, an inheritance or an insurance settlement can rattle the normal flow of life and create a multitude of options and choices on how to best apply the newly found money. Even new found money can mess up a normal lifestyle. ("Dear God, let it happen to me!")

The first step in creating a comfortable financial life is to know where the money is going. Figuring out the income side of cash flow is easy, while figuring out the expense side is difficult. Everyone knows almost to the penny how much income flows into the household on a weekly or monthly basis. The sources of income are usually very identifiable. Salaries, commissions, rental income, interest and dividends, etc. are generally easy to peg, making it easy to gauge our lifestyle, or at least how our lifestyle should look.

The expenses are another matter! I have had a number of meetings with both singles and married couples about their budgeting issues. At these appointments I usually pull out a cash flow sheet which lists the income sources on the top of the page and a list of typical expenses on the bottom three-fourths of the page (see example below). The list includes items such as rent or mortgage, food (groceries and eating out), gasoline, clothes, etc. The list also includes items that many people only think of occasionally such as Christmas or birthday gifts, vacations, cable TV, hobbies, health club dues, etc. These can be very fascinating appointments as we go down the list of expenses one by one.

Category	Current Monthly Actual Average	Future Monthly Target (1 Month)	Future Monthly Target (1 Year)
I. Income Sources			
-Salary #1			
-Salary #2			
-Bonuses & Commissions			
-Business Income (net)			
-Interest & Dividends			
-Real Estate (net)			
-Other Misc.			
SUBTOTAL			

It's Not What You Earn, It's What You Keep

Category	Current Monthly Actual Average	Future Monthly Target (1 Month)	Future Monthly Target (1 Year)
II. Outflow Expenses			
Tax Deductible			
-Property Tax			
-Mortgage Interest			
-Charitable Donations			
-Medical & Dental			
-Tax Preparation			
-State Income Tax			
-Other Misc.			
General			
-Food /Groceries /Meals			
-Clothing			
-Utilities			
-Home Maintenance & Furnishings			
-Telephone			
-Auto Maintenance & Gas			
-Entertainment			
-Vacations			
-Dues & Subscriptions			
-Gifts			
-Mortgage Principal or Rent			
-Auto Loan Payments #1			
-Auto Loan Payments #2			
-Personal Hygiene & Dry Cleaning			
-Other Misc.			
Special			
-FICA (Social Security)			
-Federal Income Tax			
-Home owners/ Renters Insurance			
-Auto/Boat Insurance			
-Life Insurance			
-Health Insurance			
-Disability/ Liability Insurance			

Category	Current Monthly Actual Average	Future Monthly Target (1 Month)	Future Monthly Target (1 Year)
-Credit Card Payments			
-Loan Payments			
-Savings & Investments			
-Other Misc.			
SUBTOTAL			
III. Net Discretionary Income (Income – Outflow)			

Finally after about 20 minutes the cash flow sheet is filled out and down at the bottom of the page I will subtract the total expenses from the total income. If there is a negative number, we have at least identified the problem and the cause of stress. But rarely does this happen! About 95% of the time, we end up with a positive number. The conversation usually goes something like this. I'll say, "Well, according to your numbers, it looks like you have about $380 left over each month, after expenses". After a few seconds of silence and a surprised stare, they respond, "You have got to be kidding, that can't be possible!"

"I didn't make these numbers up. I just recorded what you gave to me." I report.

"Well something is wrong, that can't be right." They sigh.

It is at this point of the conversation that I drop my first little bomb shell. "Then it is obvious that we now know that you do not have a handle on where your money is being spent. It is falling though the cracks and you have to figure out where!"

Find the Missing Money!

The prospects usually look bewildered, but now I have their attention. I know from experience where to begin the search for the missing money. Usually I begin by asking about their eating habits. Why? Because Americans now eat over 50% of their meals outside of the home. For meals inside the home, we normally have a handle on the expenses. Easily we can identify how much we spend on groceries each week. Outside meals are another matter. Most people do not add up the weekly cost of eating out. In 95% of the cases we spend way more than we think we do. Because of this fact, most people can cut their expenses down by simply eating at home more often. Not only does it save food costs, but you do not drive your car to your kitchen table and neither do you tip the cook. (However, complimenting the cook can go a long way!)

For people with serious cash shortfalls, I explore their lifestyle habits, which can be a dangerous thing. Most people think they deserve the lifestyle they have chosen and by my questioning it, feathers can be ruffled. But I do it anyway, because these people are actually paying me to tell them the truth. This is not a popularity contest, so I just keep plowing for answers.

Once they have discovered that they really don't know where they are spending all their money, I will offer a few suggestions to help them. First, I give them a homework assignment to sit down for an hour and look through their checkbook and credit card statements for at least the last three months. Then they are to categorize all the ways the money is used or spent. I remember once doing this for myself and was very surprised to discover we were spending an average of $92.00 per month on pizza delivery! Yes, we had two teenage kids and both my wife and I were working, but that was a shocker to discover we were spending

$1,000 per year to order pizza, plus tips! A simple solution would be to cook cheese omelets or have soup and sandwiches at least once per week. Our pizza budget would be cut in half! The "extra" money could go towards the clothing budget or another more helpful place.

Once the categories are filled out, then they simply total the numbers and compare with the total income column. I warn the people not to cheat, but to write down everything. We all forget that we go out to eat a lunch at the mall and run by the store and pick up some socks for $6.00. While there, we see a nice looking belt and decide that would really look nice around my waist. Cost? $18.00. While paying for the goods, a sweet smell of chocolate covered peanuts drifts across our nostrils, so we drop $4.00 on a half-pound of goodies. Counting the $10.00 lunch, we just spent $38.00 in less than one hour with $14.00 going for food and $24.00 going for clothes. Note that the belt and the peanuts were not currently necessary nor on a budgeted priority list which means $22.00 was spent unnecessarily. Are peanuts and belts bad? No, but they are not necessary in this month's budget and cash flow.

Sometimes people will squirm when I challenge their life style. In the past I've asked a couple with cash flow problems, "How much do each of you spend monthly on cell phones?"

"Oh, about $110 per month." they responded.

"How old are you?" I asked.

"I'm 41 and my wife is 39." He responded, with a puzzled look.

"I'm betting you both have had cell phones for four years, so I have a question: How did you manage to survive getting along without cell phones for 36 or 37 years of your life?", I asked, never cracking a smile.

They giggled back to me, "I don't know."

They smiled, but they got my point. Is anything wrong with cell phones? No, they are very convenient. However, if this couple is sinking quickly into debt and emotionally stressing because of it, they need to wake up and survive the inconvenience of not having cell phones for a while until their cash flow improves. The same thing would apply to the other lifestyle conveniences such as cable TV, magazine subscriptions, brand new cars and health spa memberships.

I remember once meeting with a lovely middle-aged couple who was experiencing major league debt and cash flow problems. They had two children and they both had good paying jobs, but the credit card debt was crushing them. I knew after looking closely at their expenses that they were out of control. I always try to shoot straight with people because by the time they call me, I know there have been many arguments and fights over the money problems. By being an objective third party advisor, I can usually say things to each spouse without them throwing something at me.

With this particular couple I noticed that the wife was very attractive, tanned and obviously in good shape. On her expense list was an item called "health spa" for $98 per month. This couple, mind you, was "in the red" several hundred dollars a month and feeding their credit cards like there was no limit. I looked her right in the eye and smiled and suggested, "Why don't you put on shorts and a tank top, jog over to the local high school track and run stadium stairs on these warm spring days. A few calisthenics and you will be just as tanned and buffed, for free!" That simple idea would save them $1,200 per year or $100 per month and the $100 could be used towards paying down one of the 15 credit cards on the list.

She looked at me like I just told her to sell one of her kids to raise money! Since I was on a roll, I suggested they drop the cell phones, cable TV, club dues, eating out for dinner five times per week and this would save them $600 per month which would help whittle down their $45,000 in credit card debt. Budget and cash flow meetings get very personal sometimes.

Identifying the "red flags" in the expense column is critical to successful cash flow management. We all got along in years past without certain conveniences before we had our current income. Human nature tends to turn a convenience into a "right" after awhile. This can be dangerous.

Plastic Money and Credit Cards Can Become a Curse Rather Than a Convenience!

Many people use the credit card as a savings account. Big mistake! Every person should "squirrel away" at least three to six months' worth of monthly expenses for emergency use. Park the money in an interest bearing money market account, even if the interest rate is low. This is not an investment account, nor a checking account. Banks would love for you to park the cash in a short term CD, however, there are early withdrawal penalties. Do not allow plastic money to reduce the pain of not spending. It is a trap! When you pull out cash or write a check there is an emotional imprint locked on your brain that the swiping of a plastic card through a slot does not do. Be cautious and keep only enough cards for emergency use only. If a card is used, make every effort to pay it off quickly and immediately. Make it a priority, for delaying the pay off will cost you money.

If you are in serious debt there are several steps to attacking the problem. Numbers do not lie. Write down on a list each debt, the interest rate and the minimum monthly payment. Rate the debts according to interest rate with the highest interest rate getting assigned #1 and so on. If there are very small debts of say one hundred or two hundred dollars, rank these as #1A, #1B, etc. Now prioritize the numbers. You should pay off the small (#1A and #1B) first for psychological reasons. Debt brings despair. You need a couple of quick victories and paying off these small debts feels good. Eliminating an emotional barrier to success is important. Next, overload money towards the highest interest debts first and foremost because these debts are draining your cash flow more than the others. Pay something on all of your debts each month, but pay a greater percentage of the high interest and less on the low or no interest debt. Also call each creditor and ask them to lower the interest rate too. Tell them you will pay the debt off, but you are struggling financially and need some relief. Some creditors will likely respond to your plea and help you.

Simultaneously, as described earlier, begin to eliminate or lower all unnecessary expenses. This will be painful, but debt is even more painful especially if you start getting nasty phone calls from angry creditors. Once you have things in better shape, your cash flow improves and the freed up cash accelerates your debt payments. Only then can you return to some of the lifestyle items you gave up. Remember, sacrifice is only temporary.

I remind my clients that drowning is not a relative thing. If your nose stays two inches below the surface of the water or one hundred feet below, you will still drown. Whether your debt is great or small, you are going "in the hole" every month and you will eventually drown financially. Be cautious and alert always about debt and cash flow – always!

Should a person ever declare bankruptcy? Not unless financial disaster has left an impossible situation. Bankruptcy looks like an easy way out when the emotional pain of debt and cash flow shortages are crushing the spirit in a person. However, you have to count the cost! You may not be able to borrow money for a home or car for years to come after declaring bankruptcy, not to mention the emotional guilt and shame it may cause.

On a happier note, if your cash flow is under control with your expenses in check, this allows you to plan and develop goals for the future. Whether short term or long term; there is an improvement in your quality of life upon reaching financial goals. Goals such as a new house, new car or furniture are possible. Education plans for kids become a reality with proper cash flow management. Most of all freedom is achievable, both emotionally and financially if your cash flow is generally positive.

It is important to note that cash flow management has nothing to do with how much money a person makes or the size of their net worth. Many of my counseling sessions regarding cash flow and debt are with people making well over $100,000 per year. The question is more about lifestyle and so is the answer: live within your means. Whether wealthy or of modest means, your control of cash flow will determine ultimately if you are content or stressed out. Learn the lessons well, for they will benefit you the rest of your life.

"Owe nothing to anyone, except to love one another"
Apostle Paul (Romans 13:8)

Notes

_____

_____

_____

_____

_____

_____

_____

_____

_____

_____

_____

_____

_____

_____

"Money is a terrible master but an excellent servant."
(Phineas Taylor Barnum)

"Most people are more concerned with the return of their money more than with the return on their money."
Will Rogers

Chapter 4

Protecting Your Assets

Sometimes when we speak at seminars, we remind everyone that there are two objectives in regards to wealth: one is to increase your assets and the other is to preserve your assets. Preservation and protection should always be a goal of your financial planning. Sometimes this goal can be achieved easily but often it is more complex. This chapter will explore the many facets of preserving and protecting your assets.

Risk of Losing Important Documents

Every document has an "expiration date." Credit card statements and receipts need to be kept at least a year or longer, especially if the credit card is used for purchases that are deductible. Credit card companies will charge for copies if you have to have them reproduced.

Tax records from the IRS need to be kept a minimum of three years, but sometimes tax records need to be kept longer. Income tax preparation requires information on tax deductions; good record keeping substantiates tax deductions. In addition, copies of bills and receipts are necessary in case of errors. Maintaining good records could shorten the time it takes to clean up a mistake or even collect benefits such as life insurance proceeds and military benefits. Creating and keeping a "paper trail" is always advisable.

Will: Protecting Assets After Death

Protecting your assets is just as important at death as when you are living. Having a will ensures your assets will go to your family properly after death. For some reason, we all treat death as something that will never happen or is at least a long way off.

Unfortunately, death is inevitable!

John Denver went out for a routine plane ride. He crashed and died. He left three children, no will and a 20 million dollar estate, which probably created for his beneficiary a financial nightmare in addition to the emotional trauma.

While you may not have a 20 million dollar estate, it is important that you take control of your legacy. Thousands of Americans die "intestate" each year, meaning without a will. If you want the Clerk of Court in your county to use the laws of your state to handle your asset distribution, then simply die without a will. A will is a document that transfers property at your death to named beneficiaries that you control. The goal here is to distribute your property to those whom you choose. A will is also used to name guardians for your children, if they are under 18 years of age. Underage children can unfortunately become a battleground for the relatives if both mom and dad die accidentally at the same time. You do not want that nightmare to happen!

A will must be in writing, signed by you, and have two witness's notarized signatures (some states require three). We recommend hiring an experienced attorney to do your will. Your will should also be reviewed every three years, or if there is a change in your family situation like a birth, divorce or a change in the tax law.

A trusted executor will need to be named in the will. The executor has a fiduciary responsibility to carry out the terms and conditions of the will and to settle all debts. If the estate is large and complex, the executor usually is paid a fee. (Estate planning is covered in detail in another chapter.) Remember, your will is the last "say-so" you have. Don't let the state or federal government "say" it for you.

Credit Risk

Your credit report or credit history is your key to financial freedom. With a good report, you can obtain credit cards, purchase a home or car. With poor credit, often times, you can't even lease a car, much less purchase one. Statistics indicate that as much as 70 percent of credit card reports contain errors. Your credit history is collected, maintained and evaluated by national reporting agencies that receive regular reports on you from companies where you have accounts. The information in your credit report may include:

➢ Name, including all variations of it
➢ Current and previous addresses and telephone numbers
➢ Date of birth
➢ Current and previous employers

- ➢ Names of creditors like banks, hospitals, landlords, utility companies, etc.
- ➢ Payment patterns
- ➢ Unpaid debt; closed bank accounts
- ➢ Public records such as tax liens, bankruptcies and judgments
- ➢ Inquiries from companies

By law, your credit report cannot contain:

- ➢ Business accounts (unless credit is in your name)
- ➢ Civil suits, judgments, records of arrest and other adverse information more than 7 years old
- ➢ Debts and paid tax liens more than 7 years old
- ➢ Gender, race or religion
- ➢ Medical history on your health
- ➢ Savings or checking account information

There are three major credit bureaus: Equifax, Experian and Transunion

All three of these credit bureaus have websites where you can find out how to obtain a free copy of your credit report. Be careful though, because sometimes you have to agree to join a credit monitoring service to get a free copy. Currently, if you are denied credit, you're entitled to a free copy. As of June 2004, the Federal Trade Commission declared a ruling that Equifax, Experian and Transunion will start allowing consumers to check there credit reports at no cost every 12 months.

A suggestion that will help you protect your credit is to opt out of junk mail and telemarketing lists. To remove you name from all marketing lists, call (888)567-8688. To stop most other junk mail, write a letter to Mail Preference Services and ask to be removed from the list. The address is:

Mail Preference Services
Direct Marketing Association
PO Box 9008
Farmington, NY 11735

Include in the letter, your compete name and mailing address.

Identity Theft

What do you do if you are a victim of identity fraud? You must act quickly! Start a log of all your efforts to protect yourself. The log should include things such as:

➢ Record all conversations with your creditors
➢ Send correspondence by certified mail
➢ Keep copies of all letters and documents
➢ Contact the authorities – give them as much information as possible

A website that is useful for identity theft is: www.idtheftcenter.org. Also, there is an identity theft hotline: 877-IDTHEFT (877-438-4338).

Another important step is to put a fraud alert on your credit report. Immediately call and/or write the three agencies:

Experian
Phone: 888-397-3742
Fax: 800-301-7196
Address: PO Box 1017
              Allen, TX 75013

Equifax
Phone: 800-525-6285
Address: PO Box 740250
           Atlanta, GA 30374

Transunion
Phone: 800-680-7289
Address: PO Box 6790
           Furrerton, CA 92634

If your credit cards are stolen, *CALL YOUR CREDITORS IMMEDIATELY!*

If your checks are stolen, *NOTIFY YOUR BANK IMMEDIATELY!* Close the accounts. Contact the check verification companies, DO NOT rely on the bank to do this.

Checkrite: 800-766-2748
Chexsystems: 800-428-9623
Crosscheck: 800-522-1900
Equifax: 800-437-5120
National Processing: 800-526-5380
Scan: 800-262-7771
Telecheck: 800-710-9898

Even if you are a victim of a crime and checks get returned, for insufficient funds, etc., you may be prevented from opening an account at another bank for up to 5 years.

If your ATM or debit card is stolen, *CONTACT YOUR BANK IMMEDIATELY!* Get new cards and new passwords.

If you are victim to a fraudulent change of address, *NOTIFY POSTAL INSPECTOR IMMEDIATELY!*

If you Social Security number is misused, *CALL SOCIAL SECURITY IMMEDIATELY!* 800-772-1213 or www.ssa.gov

The bottom line on protecting your self is to safeguard all of your information. Be careful of what you put into a computer or give out over the phone without absolutely positively knowing who is on the other end.

Insurance to Protect Against Risk

Some Insurance salespeople would lead you to believe that life insurance is the answer for every financial need. Insurance is to protect you against a financial loss only.

Losses in themselves cannot be prevented, but suffering financial loss can!

So to protect yourself against financial loss of property, life or disability, you can insure it. Please refer to our chapter on Insurance for more details and advice.

Auto plus Homeowners Insurance protects some of your most valuable assets: your car and home plus its contents. Life insurance covers another valuable asset: yes, your life! Even more, it is actually a way to protect future earnings potential for your family. Given the importance of insurance and what it protects, policies should be kept in a fireproof safe at home and you should also maintain a list of these policies in a safe deposit box.

For most of us, our largest asset until retirement years is the ability to earn an income. Having disability insurance is more important than life, health, homeowners or auto insurance during the earning years. If disability is not offered through your employer, do some research and put a plan in place.

Health insurance is a concern for all whether employed or retired. The rising cost of healthcare makes health insurance coverage a necessity. If you become unemployed, you are entitled to Cobra (Congressional Budget Reconciliation

Act) for up to 18 months. You must pay the full premium, but at group rates that are sometimes cheaper than individual rates. You are also entitled to Cobra benefits if you are a widow, widower or child of an employee who dies while working for the same company 3 or more years, you are the divorced spouse or child of an employee and have not reached 23.

One other important point to make about health insurance is that if you are unemployed for a minimum of 12 weeks you may withdraw from an IRA to make health insurance premium payments without incurring a penalty.

Consumer information on various health insurance plans is available from the following:

> American Association of Health Plans
  www.aahp.org
  (202)778-3200
> Life and Health Foundation for Education
  www.life-line.org
  (202)464-5000

If you plan on retiring prior to age 65, health insurance should be a concern as well. Unless you have health insurance as a retirement benefit from a company or the government, you will need to consider your options. Cobra is available and so are individual policies. My recommendation is to get with a good financial planner and discuss deductibles, premiums, coverage, HMO's and PPO's. Higher deductibles in exchange for co-pays for doctor visits may be the answer. Of course, the status of your health is a consideration. Plan carefully before you decide to retire early.

Once you reach 65, a Medigap policy is a must to cover areas not protected by Medicare. Legislation has standardized this insurance into 10 plans. They are referred to as letters A-J. All plans offer some coverage for what is not covered in part A & B of Medicare. Shop around and use resources such as www.medicare.gov and the Center for Medicare Services at (877)267-2323.

A new concept that Congress passed could impact us all, and that concept is the Health Savings Account. On December 8, 2003, President George Bush signed into law the Health Savings Account Bill. The HSA is a tax sheltered savings account similar to the IRA, but earmarked for medical expenses only. Deposits are 100% tax deductible for the self employed and can be withdrawn to pay medical bills with tax free dollars. Employees fund it with pre-tax dollars, similar to a 401(k) plan. What is not used from the account each year stays in the account and continues to earn interest on a tax deferred basis.

When combined with a low cost, high deductible health insurance policy (required), the HSA is meant to replace a traditional high cost health insurance policy. A Health Savings Plan will restore a high degree of freedom of choice by allowing you to choose your own physician (typically from an extensive PPO directory). The HSA should be used to pay smaller covered medical expenses until the deductible is met. Should the need arise, the high deductible insurance policy takes care of covered medical expenses exceeding the deductible. You can find more information on HSA's by going to www.msainfo.net. The key advantage to the HSA is the much lower premium payment for the insurance coverage.

The final important insurance issue is life insurance (see chapter on Insurance for further description). Cash value life insurance policies offer both a death benefit (money paid to your heirs at death) and a potential return on investment. However, according to a study by the Consumer Federation of America, it takes five years before one of these policies shows a positive return, and even then, that return can be extremely small. Even after 10 years, the average return is only about 2%. I also see clients with large cash values (Ex. $46,000 of cash value for a $50,000 death benefit).

Sample Policy
    $50,000 death benefit
  – $46,000 cash value
    $ 4,000 liability to the insurance company

If you are retired and have such a policy, you are potentially better off to transfer the cash value to an investment vehicle designed to give you income now or later and avoid any additional insurance charges. You must consider the tax consequences and your insurance needs. However, tax free exchanges are allowed between life insurance and annuities. On this same note, many people have old universal life policies (see insurance chapter for definition) that may soon run out of cash value because of falling interest rates over the years. "Get an insurance check-up!" Preferably this should happen with a financial planner who is licensed in life insurance, not an insurance agent who calls himself a "financial planner." You need an objective view point.

Variable life policies should be reviewed annually for performance as well. In these policies, mutual fund type accounts are the investment options. These contracts do provide a death benefit. This is protection for your family, so please be careful regarding investment choices. Ask for an in force illustration from your agent periodically. This will give you somewhat of a look into the future concerning your policy.

Another important insurance to briefly touch on is that of long term care. Having a long term care policy in place is important in protecting your assets. When considering long term care insurance, examine your needs such as, "If I did go into a facility, how long could I pay before running out of money?" If that time frame is 10 years or less, you will need long term care protection. Keep in mind if you are married, you need to calculate this on both spouses. Your cash flow should be able to sustain the premium payments also. There are many ways to fund long term care now such as using life insurance or annuities. Contact a knowledgeable financial planner.

Insurance is all about protecting "tomorrows" today!

Investment Risk

Protecting your assets also includes risks taken by investing.

No one knows the future, except God!

So, one method of protecting yourself is through diversification or asset allocation. We encourage clients to consider balanced portfolios with both stocks, mutual funds, cash, real estate and bonds. "Diversify...diversify...diversify" is our motto.

Secondly, a key element to controlling "risk" is evaluating your personal risk tolerance. Just as one can be too conservative, one can also be too aggressive. In 2000-2002, sharp downward volatility occurred in the stock market for three consecutive years! A number of investors experienced large losses. There can be substantial risk in investing too aggressively. Most individuals invest based on past performance, which seems reasonable, but the problem is this: past performance does not guarantee future results. You should take into consideration your goals and objectives for your assets now as well as the future. Give some thought to how fluctuation in your portfolio will impact you emotionally as well as financially. Market fluctuations are normal and exiting, but at the first sign of trouble, what will be your reaction? It is important to settle on an investment plan that is diversified and has your goals in mind, with risk tolerance pre-determined. To repeat it again, find a good advisor and stay the course designed for you.

Emotional Attachment to Investments and Children

It is perfectly okay to love your children and enjoy your investments, but not to the point that you risk your financial future. Desiring to leave an inheritance to your children is fine and normal; however, living on less to help your kids is not. Position yourself to live comfortably and if something remains in the end, great! You can even consider leaving your children real estate or your business so that liquid investments can be used while you are living, but do not fund your children's wishes and then later send yourself to the poor-house.

Always be willing to seek advice and change things if necessary to protect your assets and your future. Stay the course and be wise. Monitor your finances and assets regularly, not obsessively. Be open to change; expect the unexpected.

Notes

"Money and success don't change people; they merely amplify what is already there."
(Will Smith)

"If thee marries for money, thee surely will earn it."
Ezra Bowen

Chapter 5

Marriage, Divorce & Pre-Nups

An unfortunate reality in our culture today is divorce. Approximately 50% of all marriages in America will ultimately end in divorce. Not only is divorce a highly emotional issue, but divorce always involves a division of assets. There is a major financial impact with every divorce, and the division of assets is not the only issue either.

What about the children? What about the future of their financial well being? What about the future college costs? The lives and futures of more than just the husband and wife are impacted by divorce.

Many states have tried to eliminate some of the ill will and emotion from divorce cases by creating a concept called equitable distribution. The concept is to remove the blame from the case. In other words, maybe one spouse had an affair and everyone emotionally wants to blast that wandering spouse, especially in the pocket book. Equitable distribution rules imply that the fault for the divorce should not carry so much weight, but that each spouse should end up approximately 50%/50% in the financial department. Easier said than done!

Difficulties will still arise regardless of the law. Rarely do both spouses have equal salaries or incomes. How does one fairly make a non-working spouse financially equal to a high salaried spouse, especially if the non-working spouse has not been employed for 20 years? How does a set of attorneys or a judge come up with the perfect payment of alimony to insure that the lesser income spouse is fairly treated? How do you fairly divide a business that is jointly owned by the divorcing spouses?

Even more difficult sometimes is making sure that all the assets and incomes are accounted for and are on the table for negotiation. When clients come to our office to discuss divorce settlements, we usually visit with them for the first time either during their divorce negotiations or just after they have completed the negotiations. Usually we ask a number of questions to try to get an accurate picture of the finances. Occasionally the unfortunate spouse in our office has not gotten the best end of the deal. Once we had a client whose ex-spouse had not revealed that he had an old pension plan that was going to pay him a tidy income once he reached age 65. She had already signed off on the divorce papers! Another unfortunate example was a client whose husband had charged their joint credit cards up to the maximum limit and after the divorce settlement he had conveniently skipped town and no one knew where he was located. Guess who the credit card companies pursued to get the delinquent loans paid? Our advice is to make sure through careful research and investigation that all the financial data is present and accounted for before any meaningful negotiations or settlements are signed.

One Spouse Rules!

This brings up a parenthetical point of importance. We see too many couples where one spouse is in complete control of all financial accounts and financial decisions. Sometimes it is the husband and sometimes it is the wife. This is not a healthy situation for either spouse. The emotional stress and burden of financial decision making should not be shouldered by one spouse. Likewise, the information on finances that some uninformed spouses lack can be a dangerous situation. One spouse may have generated major credit card debt while the other spouse is clueless. Another case may have one spouse with some investments that the other spouse is not aware of. Communication is the key to marital financial success. Each spouse needs to know what is going on financially inside the marriage. If marriage was a business partnership, each partner would be making a grave mistake to ignore what is going on financially within the business.

Another serious area to be reviewed carefully in a divorce is the children. First the cash flow needs to be carefully evaluated. The higher income spouse typically needs to create enough cash flow to maintain a reasonable lifestyle for the children. Child support is typically the way to offset any cash flow shortage. Child support is a non-taxable event. Alimony however, is a taxable event. The spouse paying alimony is allowed to deduct the payments from their taxable income. The spouse receiving the alimony is receiving taxable income and must report it. For a divorced spouse who is in a very high tax bracket and divorcing a non-working spouse, it makes sense, for tax purposes, to maximize the alimony payments and minimize the child support payments.

Retirement plans are important assets in a divorce settlement. If one spouse has a pension and payments will be received later in life, there needs to be a projection of future income. Of course there is going to be a judgment call as to how long a person may be expected to live. The spouse not receiving the pension should be compensated for surrendering the right to future income or should be left with joint and survivor benefits on the pension plan. Other retirement plans such as 401(k)'s, 403(b)'s or IRA's are usually split 50% unless a specific time of marriage is used to negotiate a split. To move assets from a retirement plan without taxes, Qualified Domestic Relations Order (QDRO) will need to be signed by a judge and sent to the retirement plan administrator along with instructions of where to place the money into the other spouse's IRA. One very common mistake made by some divorced couples after the divorce is completed is forgetting to change their beneficiaries on their retirement plans and life insurance policies. What kind of financial and emotional mess would be created if the ex-spouse received a couple of hundred thousand dollar IRA or death benefit, while perhaps a new spouse receives nothing?

Life insurance beneficiaries are important. Children in particular should be considered carefully in a divorce settlement. What happens if the spouse who is paying alimony or child support suffers a pre-mature death? How would the ex-spouse with the children replace the income? A simple solution would be a $150,000 to $250,000 life insurance policy on the life of the person paying alimony or child support. The parent with the children receiving the cash flow should be the owner of the policy. Why? The owner can change the beneficiary, so in case there is some emotional "bad blood" between the two spouses, the owner should be the spouse with children for protection purposes. Who should pay the premium? In a perfect world there should be enough money paid to the owner of the policy through either alimony or child support to pay the life insurance premium.

Because of being emotionally strung out, a person going through a divorce can make some mistakes, even with good legal counsel. The truth is that some attorneys are not financially savvy. A professional financial advisor may be an important addition to the divorce "team." Before signing a non-revocable legal agreement regarding money and assets, why not receive some impartial, unbiased financial input to safeguard the final decision from a qualified financial advisor?

Sometimes a spouse going through an emotionally charged divorce can simply be worn down by the battle. After a long battle with cash flow getting tighter and tighter, a person can become weary and simply cave in and give up. This can be a serious mistake and the decisions made could lead to a life of regret. Financial well being is directly tied to a good sound decision-making process. Settling a divorce successfully is no exception.

Divorce is never easy or simple. The bottom line is to find sound legal and financial advice, gather all pertinent information and then make the best and most fair decision possible. There is no perfect settlement, so once the agreement is reached and signed, move on to the next phase of your life. The future can always be better than the present.

Pre-Nups are Sexy

While we are on the subject of divorce, millions of people are re-married after going through a divorce. On top of that, many of these marriages bring together couples who have children from a previous marriage. Blended families can and do work, but we also are creating a potential "can of worms" if something goes wrong, especially in the financial arena.

We have seen many families in second marriages come unglued after the marriage has been in place for only a short time. The "love" and emotions of Mom and Dad can only go so far in a newly created blended family.

For example, we have seen cases where the husband and wife each have a house, separately owned, with original children living in their respective houses. Whose house does the couple keep for the new blended family and whose house is sold, leaving some kids obligated to move? Tough question! What does the couple do with the equity from the newly sold house – pay off mortgages and credit card debt of the other spouse or does the money stay in the original spouse's name? Tough question!

It can get even thornier. What if the new wife and husband want to blend everything financially but the older kids of one of the spouses decides that the new spouse is "stealing our inheritance." It happens! Tension can be very high when "blood becomes thicker than water."

How to be fair and equitable with your "new love" and your kids from the prior marriage is a tough decision to which there is no pat answer. Several different strategies may be helpful. For example, if a person is in good health, they could set up a life insurance policy with the new spouse as beneficiary while the will could be designed to leave personally owned assets to the original children. This strategy "protects" the new spouse financially while leaving the original assets to be inherited by the kids from the first marriage.

A second strategy would be to set up trusts that hold assets that are specified before death that go to named beneficiaries. For example, if the adult owned a stock portfolio, a beach house and some raw land, these assets could be re-titled in the name of a revocable trust that becomes irrevocable at death, which names the children from the first marriage as sole beneficiaries. The new house, now jointly owned, and perhaps the 401(K) plan or IRA beneficiary could be changed so that the new spouse would receive these assets at death.

An even better strategy would be to sign a pre-nuptial agreement before marriage. Yes, we understand that this idea seems so cold and businesslike. After all the man and woman are so in love and emotionally attracted, why throw cold water on the relationship? Because the pre-nuptial is literally an act of love to preserve and protect the relationship from stress later on through the years. Many of our clients have agreed to do this before marriage. The children can be cared for, inheritance wise, in a fair manner, and everyone knows going into the marriage what is happening. If the children are older, the couple can even sit down with them and tell them exactly what is happening to their Mom and Dad as well as their inheritance. A "pre-nup" is preventive medicine! We recommend an experienced attorney, even a divorce attorney, to assist the couple in executing the documents. The advantage of a divorce attorney is that he or she already knows the pitfalls of second marriages and can help you avoid them.

In second marriages, make sure all paperwork and legal documents are up to date, including beneficiaries on insurance policies and retirement plans, as well as wills and trust documents. In addition, make sure the real estate property is titled correctly. Several of our clients have discovered, after being in a second marriage for years that they were not in their spouses will, life insurance or retirement plans, as the primary beneficiary. These kinds of details must be addressed early in the marriage and even more importantly, updated later in the marriage. If they are ignored, chaos will surely happen one day in the future.

Divorce and second marriages are not simple matters. Emotions run high and feelings run deep. Assets and money become a tangible way to express love and emotions, but in the worst cases, greed can literally tear a family apart. Wise couples seek good advice before marriage, during marriage and if need be, after marriage.

Notes

_____

_____

_____

_____

_____

_____

_____

_____

_____

_____

_____

_____

_____

_____

*"Money is better than poverty, if only for
financial reasons."*
Woody Allen

Chapter 6

IRA's, Rollovers & Other Retirement Plans

The Individual Retirement Account (IRA), first created in 1974, has come a long way. The concept continues to be extremely popular today (the IRA is the holding spot for tens of billions of dollars worth of retirement assets). IRA's are now the most common final destination for all retirement plans, including 401(k)'s, 403(b)'s, SEP's, pensions, 457 Plans, and other retirement plan assets.

In fact, the IRA has proved so popular that a new version of the IRA was created in 1998. The new IRA is called the Roth IRA and the original IRA is now called the Traditional IRA. We will discuss the Roth IRA in more detail later.

The IRA offers many benefits to an investor, but there are confusing rules and regulations that Congress has slapped onto IRA's. In addition to this problem, Congress tinkers with the rules occasionally, making the average citizen very frustrated as they try to interpret the rules as they apply to them.

Originally, IRA contributions ($2,000 per year maximum) were fully deductible from taxes and everyone with earned income was eligible to participate. Today it is not so simple. Congress has decided only certain people can take tax deductions for their IRA contributions and those people cannot make over a certain income ceiling. Currently (and subject to change at any time), a married couple's annual income ceiling is $62,000 and a single person's $40,000. Even if you participate in a retirement plan at work such as a 401(k) plan, when your income is below these ceilings you can contribute to your IRA and deduct from taxes. If you do not have a retirement plan at work, you can make any amount of money and deduct your contribution to your IRA. If you are married and your spouse does not work, the non-working spouse can contribute to their IRA and deduct it, if combined annual income is below $150,000.

A very common misconception about IRA's is that the IRA is actually the investment product. This misconception has been perpetrated for years by banks and savings and loans who advertise like this: "Our IRA's are now paying 4.5%." Any right thinking person would miss the fact that the IRA is just a holding account or trust account. The truth is that almost any investment product—stocks, bonds, mutual funds, etc. is eligible for an IRA investment. The so-called IRA paying 4.5% is actually a CD paying 4.5% residing inside the IRA account. Proof? Notice the IRA 4.5% deal has a maturity date attached. It is really a CD in disguise.

We almost always recommend setting up an IRA at a brokerage firm for maximum freedom in choosing from a variety of investment vehicles. A second choice would be creating the IRA within a mutual fund family where you could easily diversify among any number of different mutual funds. Mutual funds make it convenient to contribute monthly into the IRÁ by a bank draft. The strategy, called Dollar-Cost-Averaging, allows for consistent contributions to be spread over the year instead of rushing to make a lump sum contribution just before the April 15th deadline.

A major advantage of IRA's, just like all qualified retirement plans is that the assets grow tax deferred. No taxes are paid until withdrawals are made, normally during retirement. This means that no capital gains are ever taxable on assets inside the IRA. This makes investment decisions much easier since no tax issues interfere with buying and selling assets. Once you begin to take income from IRA accounts, this triggers an income tax. The tax bracket will depend on your personal tax bracket during retirement. The original theory behind IRA's was that your tax deductible contributions came during your working years when you were in a higher tax bracket, while your IRA withdrawals come later during retirement when you are in a lower tax bracket. Of course this assumes that Congress will not change the tax brackets along the way, a bad assumption indeed!

Congress also sets tax standards regarding IRA and retirement plan withdrawals. If you withdraw IRA income before age 59.5, you must pay an additional 10% tax penalty on top of the ordinary income tax. Even though this penalty is severe, millions of Americans take qualified retirement plans and IRA monies and spend it on cars, furniture, or to pay off debt before the age of 59.5. It is a major mistake to do so. For example, let's assume you have $20,000 in an IRA or 401(k) and you are 40 years old, in a 40% state and federal combined income tax bracket:

$$\begin{array}{r} \$20{,}000 \text{ withdrawal} \\ \underline{\text{x } 40\% \text{ tax bracket + penalty}} \\ \$\ 8{,}000 \text{ taxes due} \end{array}$$

Your actual payout is going to be only $12,000 or 60% of your original value. Is it worth losing $8,000 to buy a new couch? Not only is it not worth the loss of money, remember that this same $8,000 could remain in the IRA for years compounding tax free. Suppose this 40 year old retired at age 65 and the IRA assets averaged an annual return of 8%. How much would the $8,000 be worth today? $54,800. Even after taxes, if the retiree were in a 20% combined tax bracket during retirement, the cash received would yield $43,800. Taking the money and running before age 59.5 is usually a serious mistake.

Congress also decided that you cannot postpone the IRA withdrawals forever!

At age 70.5 you are required to begin withdrawing money from the IRA's and retirement plans. The required minimum distribution (RMD) is based upon a formula. Current law mandates a 3.6% withdrawal in the year one turns 70.5 years of age. The 3.6% withdrawal is based on the prior year's IRA value on December 31st. For example:

$$\begin{array}{r} \$100{,}000 \text{ Value last December 31} \\ \underline{\text{x} \qquad 3.6\%} \\ \$3{,}600 \text{ RMD} \end{array}$$

You are allowed to withdraw more than 3.6% -- all the way up to 100%. But it is all fully taxable. Each year the percentage withdrawal increases based upon mortality charts. The dollar amount changes each year because the December 31 value will change, as well. If you do not comply with the required minimum distribution there is a severe penalty (50%) on the money not taken from the IRA.

If a person dies before the IRA is fully liquidated the IRA rules allow several choices for the beneficiaries. These rules were changed for the better in 2002. The primary choices before 2002 and still in effect today are:

> ➢ If you are a spouse of the deceased, you can transfer 100% of the assets from the deceased's IRA to your IRA tax free.
> ➢ If you are not a spouse, but are the beneficiary, you can simply liquidate the IRA 100% and pay the income taxes.
> ➢ The beneficiary could choose to withdrawal the money from the IRA over a 5 year period, spreading the tax bite over time and maybe keeping the income low enough not to bump them into a higher tax bracket.

Now there is a more favorable way to withdraw IRA assets as a beneficiary. If you leave the IRA in the deceased person's name and re-title it to include you as beneficiary, the withdrawals can be taken based upon the required minimum distribution at your age. This means of course a much lower RMD since most beneficiaries are much younger than the deceased. Also this could mean that more income will be received out of the IRA over the lifetime of the beneficiary and with less negative tax impact. Imagine an IRA growing an average of 7-10% annually, but because of the age of the beneficiary, the beneficiary is only taking out 1-4% up to age 59.5. The IRA assets could be quite large compared to the values at the date of the original owner's death.

One of the most useful reasons to have an IRA is that it can receive rollovers and transfers from other qualified retirement plans such as 401(k)'s and pensions. For this reason, an IRA could house the largest investment asset a person ever owns. Rollovers can occur only once annually from an IRA and the withdrawal must be placed in a new IRA within 60 days or taxes are due. A more common and simpler way to move money into an IRA is by a transfer. Transfers are unlimited between retirement plans and IRA's.

Most corporate retirement plans require paperwork or telephone PIN numbers to transfer assets into a personal IRA. Transfer papers are available at the Human Resources Department or Plan Administrator's office of the former employer.

A common sight in our office is a prospective client with two, three or even five old 401(k)'s and IRA's spread all over the place. Multiple statements every quarter cram the mailboxes and make proper diversification very difficult. We have seen clients that had identical mutual funds in 4 different retirement plans, which means they are paying annual fees on each separate IRA plan. Consolidate, consolidate, consolidate ... this is our cry!

Sometimes a person gets "down sized" or laid off in their 50's, before they are prepared to retire, and they need income in order to live. The IRS has a special policy called the rule of 72(t) that allows a person before the age of 59.5 to withdraw IRA income but not be required to pay the 10% penalty. The IRA allows three methods to determine the distribution allowed, which is based on the age of the IRA owner, the value of the IRA assets and the projected return. Once the amount of the IRA distribution is agreed upon, it cannot change for at least 5 years or until age 59.5, whichever is longer. So a 52 year old will take an equal amount of withdrawals each year until 59.5 before changing, where as a 57 year old must not change the IRA withdrawals for 5 years until age 62.

Keep in mind that certain rules such as 72(t) do not apply to other retirement plans. Likewise, certain rules apply to 401(k) plans and not to IRA's. For example, you cannot borrow or take loans against an IRA like you are allowed in a 401(k) plan. All withdrawals from IRA's before age 59.5 are considered premature distributions unless the distribution is returned within 60 days. Exceptions are withdrawals due to death, disability, first-time home purchase or college education up to $10,000.00.

Roth IRA

As mentioned earlier, there is a relatively new IRA on the investment scene called the Roth IRA. The Roth IRA is a flip side of the traditional IRA. The contributions to the Traditional IRA can sometimes be tax deductible while the Roth IRA contributions cannot. The assets in both types of IRA's grow tax deferred. The distributions from a Traditional IRA are income taxable while the distributions after age 59.5 in a Roth IRA are never taxed.

The income ceiling rules are much more investor friendly for the Roth IRA than the Traditional IRA. A single person can contribute to a Roth IRA if their annual income is less than $95,000 and a married couple under $150,000. This more flexible rule allows many people who are funding 401(k)'s or 403(b)'s at work to be able to fund Roth IRA's as well. One idea we like to remind clients of is how to use the Roth IRA for a goal other than retirement. Suppose a couple wants to pay off their home mortgage a few years before retiring? After age 59.5 the couple can withdraw up to 100% of their Roth IRA tax free, and then pay off all or part of their mortgage.

There is an interesting relationship between the traditional IRA and the Roth IRA. It is possible to transfer money between the two. The IRS allows a person to transfer money or assets such as stocks or mutual funds from the traditional IRA to the Roth IRA. There is a catch however; the transfer is a taxable event! Since the traditional IRA money and assets have never been taxed, the transfer to the Roth IRA is taxable, but is not subject to a 10% penalty. Congress, however, in all their wisdom has a caveat for this type of IRA transfer. If you earn more than $100,000 annually you will not be allowed to accomplish this type of IRA transfer. Suppose you transfer assets to a Roth IRA from a traditional IRA, and later discover you make too much money? The IRS rules allow you to return assets or cash from the Roth IRA to the traditional IRA, as long as it is before you file your tax return.

Current law allows maximum contributions to IRA's of both types are as follows:

Contribution limit (under 50 yrs old)	Over age 50	Year
$3,000	$3,500	2003-2004
$4,000	$4,500	2005
$4,000	$5,000	2006-2007
$5,000	$6,000	2008+

IRA's are one of the most useful tools available for today's investors. Rule changes are common, but the IRA should be part of every person's financial plan. By carefully investing assets in a properly diversified plan and by effectively using tax laws to minimize taxes, the IRA will be a key instrument for cash flow during your retirement years.

"By my calculations, my nest egg will last until I die ... of course, assuming I drink heavily, smoke two packs a day, and load up on carbs!!"

Notes

_____

_____

_____

_____

_____

_____

_____

_____

_____

_____

_____

_____

_____

"The easiest way for your children to learn about money is for you not to have any."
(Katharine Whitehorn)

"No one ever died with too much money."
Ben Feldman

Chapter 7

Protecting Your Estate: Do I Still Pay Taxes After I Die?

Ode to Taxes
Tax his cow, tax his goat;
Tax his pants, tax his coat.
Tax his crops, tax his work;
Tax his tie, tax his shirt.
Tax his chew, and tax his smoke.
Teach him taxes are no joke.
Tax his oil, tax his gas;
Tax his notes, tax his cash.
Put these words upon his tomb:
"Taxes drove me to my doom."
When he's gone, he can't relax.
He'll have to pay inheritance tax!

-Author Unknown

One of the most complex areas of financial planning is estate planning. Part of the complexity arises from the difficult and sometimes fuzzy IRS Tax Code. The

Tax Code is a maze of complicated policies, rules and regulations. This is precisely why we always recommend using an estate planning attorney along with your financial advisor to create a proper estate plan. Not just any lawyer will do; you need a specialist in this field.

Not everyone needs a sophisticated estate plan, but everyone needs at least a simple estate plan. Not having a plan in writing means that the local county clerk of court and the laws of your state will determine how your heirs will inherit the assets. No one should allow that scenario to unfold.

Wouldn't you rather be in control of your destiny rather than giving control to an arm of the government?

Yet, many wealthy people die each year without so much as having a simple will.

Let's begin with the basics. Almost everyone accumulates assets over their lifetime – some more, others less. But at death the ownership of these assets must be transferred. Since the American free enterprise system creates the opportunity to acquire and own property and assets, there must be an orderly system set up to pass the assets on at one's death. An estate plan is simply an orderly strategy to pass assets and property to a succeeding owner. This transfer of assets takes place most often at death, and can be accomplished in several ways, not just by use of the last will and testament.

First, assets can be transferred by **contract.** Examples of contractual agreements include, but are not limited to, a life insurance policy or a retirement plan such as an IRA, 401(K) plan, or a pension plan. By law, these "contracts" must have a beneficiary on the agreement. This means at death the beneficiary automatically inherits the assets on the retirement plan or the death benefit of the insurance policy. There may be tax consequences to the beneficiary, but the beneficiary still receives the assets. There may be a will involved, but it doesn't matter what the will says; the beneficiary receives the assets.

Secondly, **ownership** rights can transfer assets. For example, if you happen to live in a state where joint-owner-ship-with-right-of-survivorship rules exist (JWROS); this means that property will be automatically transferred to the surviving owner at the death of the first owner. This will occur regardless of what the deceased owner's will states. In particular this applies to ownership of real estate such as a home or a property. Most married couples own their home jointly, so when one spouse dies, the other surviving spouse now owns the property out-right. (There are a few states that allow people to own property as tenants-in-common. In these states, when one owner dies, the other surviving owner actually owns only their prearranged percent of the property; say 50% in the case of home ownership for a husband and wife.) If you and your elderly parent co-own a bank CD and your parent passed away, the survivor automatically owns the asset, regardless of what the will states. If three people jointly own a money market account and one dies, the other two automatically own the money market assets.

Finally, **the will** is used as a third method of transferring ownership of assets at death. Most attorneys today write wills that are comprehensive but general in nature. By this we mean that the will does not list every single household item, and which child or grandchild will get certain items. To do this would simply be too complicated and expensive as new grandchildren will arrive, new assets will be acquired, or if a child died unexpectedly. Attorneys prefer to allow the will to have codicils or amendments to be added, even handwritten, to make these types of adjustments. For example, if a mother wanted to have her daughter inherit her rings or jewelry rather than her son, this would be handled by adding an amendment or codicil to the will.

There is a fourth way to pass assets to heirs and this is by use of a trust. A trust can be set up for very specific reasons to accomplish very specific goals. Trusts by nature and by law must have beneficiaries and trustees. Trusts also pay taxes and can have their own Tax ID numbers. They can be set up while you are living (a Living Trust) or they can be set up at your death to control assets after you pass away, if the will specifies exact details of the trust.

Trusts are complicated, but can be very useful because they can be designed for specific goals. For example, if a parent had a child that was physically or mentally disabled, the parent could set up a trust called a "Special Needs Trust". At the death of the parent, the trust could receive assets and a pre-designated trustee could manage the assets and income generated for the benefit of the disabled child for the rest of their lives.

A more common use of a trust stems from the desire to shelter taxes that can be charged against an estate. Estate taxes are an ominous issue for wealthy individuals. The US Congress makes a complex issue more difficult by changing the estate tax laws periodically. It makes sense to have a competent financial advisor and estate attorney check on and evaluate your estate plan every two to three years just to make adjustments to the tax laws, not to mention changes in the individual's estate and family situation.

Having noted the estate tax laws and the changing nature of them, we suggest that people proceed, however, under the laws we have today (see Figure 7.1). For example, beginning in 2004 and 2005, every American will have a $1.5 million exemption from Federal estate taxes at death. Under current law this exemption will slowly increase until 2010, at which time the exemption will revert back to $1 million. Only Congress could come up with such a wacky law! Politics unfortunately plays too big a role in tax law. This law, taken at face value, inadvertently encourages people of wealth to die late in this decade so that more of their estate will remain for their heirs and not be confiscated by the Federal government! (We have instructed all of our clients who plan to die someday to do it in 2010 while there is not estate tax! No – just kidding!)

YEAR	ESTATE TAX EXCLUSION		TOP ESTATE TAX RATE
2003	$1.0 million		49%
2004	$1.5 million		48%
2005	$1.5 million		47%
2006	$2.0 million		46%
2007	$2.0 million		45%
2008	$2.0 million		45%
2009		$3.5 million	45%
2010	No Estate Tax		0%
2011	$1.0 million		55%

Figure 7.1 Estate Tax Exclusion Chart (Source: *Ernst & Young*)

Having said that, we should note that there is one trust that every married couple should possess if they have a net worth (including life insurance death benefits) over $1.5 million. This trust is called a "By-Pass Trust" or "Credit Shelter Trust". What the IRS never bothers to tell us is that when a person dies, the 2004-2005, $1.5 million exemption exists, but unless there is a trust set up to "capture" the exemption, a person could lose it forever. For example, remember our transfer rules mentioned earlier? Suppose all the assets except the car and furniture were owned jointly or by contract. Everything then would pass directly to the surviving spouse at the first spouse's death, regardless of the will. If a couple had assets of $3 million and the husband dies, the wife would inherit 100% of the assets with *no estate tax due*. Why? Because she would fall under a rule called the unlimited marital deduction, meaning there is an unlimited amount of assets that can be transferred from one spouse to another *while alive or at death*. This sounds very good at first glance, but what if the wife dies one month after her recently deceased spouse? She would then be the owner of all $3 million of assets, but only be allowed to exempt $1.5 million using her exemption. The remaining $1.5 million would be taxed to the tune of maybe 40%. The children or heirs could owe Federal estate taxes of $600,000!

The IRS does not want land or cars or houses—they want cash!

The IRS does not have a long time frame set up either. In most cases, Federal estate taxes are *due 9 months after death*. Often you see land or houses selling to "settle the estate". Pity the family who is forced into this situation because everyone bidding at the estate sale knows that the IRS is impatiently waiting for the cash of the deceased. Everyone will likely underbid for the property under such dire circumstances, leaving the heirs less money than they deserve.

Note the heirs pay the estate taxes, not the owner of the property. Children pay estate taxes, not the parents! Parents with wealth need to understand that assets accumulated by hard work and savings over a lifetime can disappear (partially) within 9 months of death if estate planning is not properly put in place. Sad to say, thousands of wealthy people in America today do not even have a will, much less a trust to protect assets.

If the "By Pass" Trust is set up properly, after the first spouse dies, up to $1.5 million of assets (life insurance death benefits, land, stocks, mutual funds, etc.) can be placed into the name of the trust, sheltering it from future estate tax consequences. If done properly, the surviving spouse is now trustee of the trust having full control of assets and income. Setting up the trust *does not mean losing control!* The wife can invest the money, live off the income and even invade the principal for her own well-being. In our example, she now controls up to $1.5 million of assets in the trust and owns the other $1.5 million out right. Should she accidentally die shortly after her husband, she takes her own $1.5 million Federal estate tax exemption. Her children or heirs receive it tax-free. Because the other $1.5 million in the trust was protecting her husband's $1.5 million exemption, the children or heirs also receive the trust assets as beneficiaries—all estate tax free! The children owe no estate taxes on the $3 million, doubling the tax free transfer of assets.

They may however, owe state death taxes. Each state has individual death tax rates and exemptions of their own. Consult an attorney or your state government tax office for local regulations and laws.

There is one other trust worth mentioning for estate planning purposes and that is the **Charitable Remainder Trust (CRT)**. The trust is an excellent vehicle to use for tax savings, and not just for one tax break, but for several tax breaks. This trust is ideal for people with highly appreciated property such as land, old stock, or a business that has been held for years.

Notice the word "charitable" is part of this trust. Eventually a charity, church or school will receive some benefit, but that comes years later. The donor to the trust will receive tremendous benefits for being charitably minded while still alive.

Not one, not two, but three different types of taxes are saved by the donor using the CRT: income taxes, capital gains taxes and estate taxes. This three-pronged tax savings plan is what makes this trust so special. The best way to explain how the CRT works is to use an example. Suppose a couple, both 60 years old, own some land that is worth $440,000 but the original purchase price was $40,000 (cost basis). If they sell the land for a $400,000 capital gain, they could owe approximately $100,000 in taxes depending on current state and federal tax rates. Most people would not sell the land for such a steep loss of money, due to taxes.

Suppose instead they created a CRT (using an advisor and an attorney) and deeded the property to the trust. The trust then sold the property for $440,000. Several amazing tax benefits happened all at once. First, because the CRT is a charitable entity, there were no capital gains taxes due upon sale. Secondly, because the gift of the land was irrevocable, there is no estate tax due on the asset at death because it is no longer in the donor's estate. And finally, since the donor gifted to "charity" they receive a partial income tax deduction. Three tax breaks with one gift is difficult to resist. But you may be saying, "They gave the land away. Who could afford to do that?"

There are additional reasons and financial benefits for giving something away to a CRT. In the trust documents, the CRT must provide income for the rest of the donor's lives; income back to the donors. By law the minimum income must be 5% per year. For our illustration, let's say the couple wants 7% cash flow for life. The trust would then be obligated to provide approximately $30,000 per year of taxable income until both donors pass away. Since the couple receives income back from the trust, the IRS will give them only a partial income tax deduction of say 50% or $220,000. If the couple cannot use all $220,000 in tax write-offs for that year against their income, no problem. They can carry forward their unused tax write off for an additional 5 years. If the donors, either one of them, live at least fifteen years, in this example they will receive all of their gift value back.

Protecting Your Estate: Do I Still Pay Taxes After I Die?

The CRT is incredibly flexible. Suppose the couple doesn't need the income for 3 more years. The trust can accumulate the annual income and pay it out later. The donors must name a charity, church or school as beneficiary at their death, but they can change the beneficiary at anytime they want up until they die.

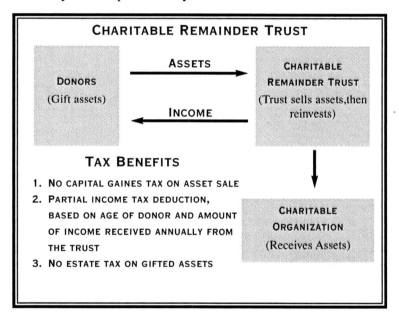

CHARITABLE REMAINDER TRUST

DONORS (Gift assets) → ASSETS → CHARITABLE REMAINDER TRUST (Trust sells assets, then reinvests) → INCOME

TAX BENEFITS
1. NO CAPITAL GAINES TAX ON ASSET SALE
2. PARTIAL INCOME TAX DEDUCTION, BASED ON AGE OF DONOR AND AMOUNT OF INCOME RECEIVED ANNUALLY FROM THE TRUST
3. NO ESTATE TAX ON GIFTED ASSETS

CHARITABLE ORGANIZATION (Receives Assets)

If you are smart, you may be saying to yourself, "I like it, but there are losers in this CRT strategy—the children just lost a $440,000 inheritance." Yes, that is true! But we could easily set up another trust called an Irrevocable Life Insurance Trust that could own a "Second to Die" policy on the couple. "How would the premiums be paid?" By the trust income of course. Assume the couple's new policy costs $4,000 per year for a $440,000 death benefit. The trust income pays the premiums and the couple still receives $26,000 cash flow until death instead of $30,000 annually. A "Second to Die" policy is on both the husband and wife and does not pay a death benefit until the second spouse dies. Once both Mom and Dad pass away the children receive their $440,000 inheritance tax free in the form of life insurance proceeds. The insurance is owned by the life insurance trust so that the death benefit is outside the estate of the donor. The beneficiaries of the life insurance trust are the children. Everybody wins, except the IRS!

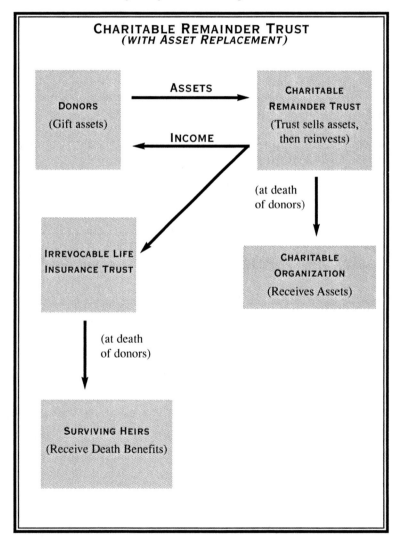

CHARITABLE REMAINDER TRUST
(WITH ASSET REPLACEMENT)

DONORS
(Gift assets)

ASSETS

CHARITABLE REMAINDER TRUST
(Trust sells assets, then reinvests)

INCOME

(at death of donors)

IRREVOCABLE LIFE INSURANCE TRUST

CHARITABLE ORGANIZATION
(Receives Assets)

(at death of donors)

SURVIVING HEIRS
(Receive Death Benefits)

One last recommendation regarding setting up a trust; the most important person in the trust is the trustee. In some cases we have seen clients whose trust assets were controlled by a bank, as the trustee. The bank was charging excessive trust fees and was not operating the trust in the best interest of the client. Be careful to choose a trustee who has your beneficiaries' best interest at heart. Also in the trust document, allow your beneficiaries the ability to fire and hire new trustees if they see fit.

Estate planning is complicated, but very valuable and beneficial for many reasons. It is worthwhile to know and understand how estate planning can save your family considerable taxes, and ease the pain of your passing.

Estate Planning Definitions

Will: A will directs where and how you want your estate property distributed when you die. Without one the county court house will decide, according to state law. A will does not control some property with contractual beneficiary designations such as life insurance benefits, retirement accounts, and trust assets.

Probate: The court process that ensures that the portion of an estate passed by a will is properly settled, including debts.

Executor(s) or Personal Representative: The person or persons who administer your final estate. The person oversees not only financial matters, such as filing a final return and distributing assets, but may have to deal with family situations.

Power-of-Attorney: This gives another person, such as your spouse or an adult child, the legal power to act financially and make decisions on your behalf should you become incapacitated. This document is in effect while you are alive and ceases when you die.

Trust: A legal entity for holding property for the benefit of the creator and the trust or other beneficiaries. Trusts are used for many reasons including confidentiality, avoiding probate or saving estate taxes.

Trustee: The person or organization, who owns, controls and manages a trust's assets.

Revocable and Irrevocable Trusts: A revocable trust means the creator of the trust can change fundamental aspects of the trust or even dissolve it. It is included in the estate. Irrevocable trusts typically are used to reduce estate taxes by moving assets from the estate. The creator typically loses some or all of the control of the assets.

Testamentary and Inter Vivos Trusts: A testamentary trust is established upon the creator's death and an inter vivos trust is established during the creator's lifetime.

Notes

_____

_____

_____

_____

_____

_____

_____

_____

_____

_____

_____

_____

_____

_____

"Money frees you from doing things
you dislike. Since I dislike doing
nearly everything, money is handy."
(Groucho Marx)

"A simple fact that is hard to learn is that the time to save money is when you have some."
Joe Moore

Chapter 8

Mutual Funds

Mutual funds are probably the most popular investment vehicle in America today. According to Morningstar, there are over 8,000 mutual funds with over 3 trillion dollars invested. Mutual funds have been around in the US since 1924.

What is a mutual fund? It is a managed account of diversified stocks or bonds or a combination of both. The manager can be an individual or a committee. The individual investor's "delegate" authority to the manager or managers to buy and sell securities and for that service, a fee is charged by the fund. There are two basic types of mutual funds. The most common is called an "open-end fund" because there is an unlimited number of shares for purchase and the fund can grow infinitely large by simply selling more shares as investors deposit their money. On the other hand, a "closed-end fund" has a finite number of shares just like common stock shares of a company. If someone buys shares of a closed-end fund then someone else has to sell shares to complete the trade. For the purpose of this chapter we will discuss the much more common open-end funds.

Advantages and Disadvantages

Mutual funds have certain advantages over individual stock ownership.

> ➢ One obvious advantage is diversification of assets. For example, you, as in investor, can purchase and own common shares of stock of any particular company. With the same money, using a mutual fund, you could purchase shares of 50, 100 or even 200 companies that the particular mutual fund might own.

> ➢ A second advantage is that you could own multiple companies of a specific type. For example, your $1,000 could own a health care sector mutual fund that might own 50 or 100 companies in the healthcare area, drug companies and HMO's. These funds are called sector funds, using company stocks of a sector of the economy.

> ➢ A third advantage is the professional manager or management team may have much more expertise, research, and insight that you may not have access to.

As with every investment or financial strategy, there are also disadvantages with owning mutual funds.

> ➢ Funds charge an annual fee for management of the assets. Also, as with ownership of stocks, there could be a commission involved in the purchase or the sale of mutual funds. Ownership of individual stocks does not normally carry an annual fee, unless you agree to pay a money manager to manage

your stocks. It is your option, but with funds there is no option on the administrative fees.

➤ A second disadvantage is in the important area of taxes. With individual stocks, you determine when to purchase and when to sell. Capital gains and capital losses, with their respective tax consequences, are all in your hands. But with mutual funds the government requires funds to declare capital gains and losses from trades within the fund each calendar year. There is potentially additional bad news on taxes. If your mutual fund had a bad year and your original investment has lost money, on paper, you still may have to pay capital gains and dividend taxes. How come? Because the internal trades within the fund could create taxable events that you pay for. There is some good news—you get credit later for taxes paid at the time you sell the fund.

Be careful, no matter when you buy the fund during the year. If there are net gains from the stocks traded by the manager inside the fund, there will be capital gains taxes to pay, even if you purchase the fund a few days before the date the fund designates you as an owner of record. You will pay capital gains taxes as if you owned it for a full year. The IRS, however, does not give you a tax break in the other direction. If there are net capital losses on the mutual fund, the investor does not get to claim them, but they are carried forward to the next calendar year to offset future gains. This means that if you sell the fund before next year's tax reporting data rolls around, you receive no benefit from the losses.

➤ Inherently there is a disadvantage to letting someone else manage your assets and that is loss of control. As a fund owner you cannot control the stocks or bonds that you own, nor can you control the tax consequences.

Choices of Funds

Believe it or not, there is one other disadvantage regarding mutual funds: there are too many choices! There are over 8,000 funds to choose from. In order to simplify the choices, the mutual fund industry has classified various types of categories of funds. For simplicity sake we will not discuss all the categories, but we will discuss the basic areas that each investor should understand.

Bond funds and stock funds are the first major division of funds. If you want to own a company and have an equity position, then stock funds are your ticket to ownership. If however, you want to own a portfolio of loans to corporations, governments or agencies, then the bond funds would be your choice. You may even decide that owning both stocks and bonds would be a great way to diversify your assets. Then the balanced fund could be your choice. Instead of owning one bond fund and another stock fund, you could simply own one balanced fund.

After you decide whether bonds and/or stocks are the best strategy to diversify your assets, then you can further break down your choices to fit very narrow and specific needs. See Figure 8.1 for some examples.

Stock Funds		Bond Funds	
TYPE	FUND CATEGORY	TYPE	FUND CATEGORY
Large Company	Large Cap, Growth & Income	Corporate Bonds	Income Funds
Mid size Company	Mid Cap	US Gov't Bonds	Gov't Bond Funds
Small Company	Small Cap	State, City, County Bonds	Municipal Bond Funds
Large Company Index	S&P 500 Index Fund	International Bonds	International Bonds
Small Company Index	Russell 2000 Index		
NASDAQ Stocks	NASDAQ Index		

Figure 8.1 *Examples of Funds*

The list goes on and on. There is almost no category of stocks and bonds that is not represented. For instance, there are sector funds that offer every "flavor" desired; everything from leisure to energy to pharmaceuticals to the Internet. There are varieties for the politically correct crowd called "green" funds or "social" funds. This book will not delve into every nook and cranny of the fund industry, but suffice it to say that virtually any asset allocation strategy can be created with the various funds.

There is one other distinction in the fund choices that should be mentioned because sometimes it is not obvious on the surface. Whether a fund opts for the "growth" philosophy or the "value" philosophy of picking stocks is not always obvious from the name of the fund. The style will take some research. Without writing a thesis on the differences between "growth" and "value" strategies, let us explore the basics of each style.

The "growth" fund manager is looking for companies that are growing very rapidly, usually faster than their peer group. The manager does not particularly pay attention to the price/earnings ratio or the corporate debt. Their focus is on growth and they do not want to miss out on this window of opportunity, even if the fund owns it only a few weeks or even days. Hence, these managers are called "momentum" managers because they buy into the momentum as the stock prices rise rapidly and sell when momentum goes negative and the price dives. At least this is the theory. Timing it correctly to catch the cycles correctly is not as easy as it seems. If it was, everybody would be doing it.

On the other hand, the "value" manager is not so concerned that he may miss out on a high-flying stock. This manager looks for "bargains", and for undervalued stocks that are currently out of favor. Maybe the company had a bad quarter or a bad year and the stock drops dramatically. A "value" manager has methodology to measure the company's intrinsic value and once the market drives the price below that level, the stock may become a candidate to purchase. Especially if the manager believes the market has over-reacted and the company has a viable future for growth or improvement.

Interestingly, the value funds and the growth funds often grow and decline cyclically in opposite directions. Recent history shows that growth funds had a great run on returns in the late 90's while value funds plundered a bit. Between 2000-2003, the growth funds took a serious hit while the value funds had a good run. Then it makes sense to have at least one value style fund and one growth style fund in your portfolio for better protection and diversification. That way, you will never be completely out of sync with the stock market cycles.

Load or No-Load

One of the distinct differences between mutual funds has nothing to do with the investments or the strategies. It has everything to do with how everyone in the management and advisory areas get paid. By nature and structure, mutual funds have other experts, involved in the investment process. All mutual funds have to pay expenses. They do not have a business in a vacuum. This business, like all others, has expenses to pay from salaries to rent to research to trading costs. Therefore, all funds have administrative expenses that are deducted from the assets of the mutual funds. For example, if the funds annual expenses are 1% annually and the fund performance resulted in a 10% growth last year, then your actual return will be slightly less than 10%.

There is another "cost" to some funds. The industry and the media call it a "load". Actually it is a form of commission. The commission can be paid in several ways. Developed a number of years ago, the funds generally have categorized commissions as either class A, B, C, or K (or actually many other alphabetical categories). Please carefully read the specific fund prospectus first for details, but generally the class breakdowns are as follows:

Class A: upfront commission 5.5% for stock funds; 4.5% for bond funds, but the commissions drop if certain break points (commission discounts) are met within a 13-month period. Note the following chart for stock funds:

Investment	Commission
$0 - $24,999	5.5%
$25,000 - $49,999	5.25%
$50,000 - $99,999	5.0%
Etc.	Etc.

Class B: Annual commissions of 1%, paid on a quarterly basis for 8 years, then it ceases. However, if you sell out of the fund family and leave the fund family, there is a declining back-end fee that begins at 5% in year one and decreases to zero in year 6. However, inside the fund family there is no back-end fee or charge for switching funds.

Class C: 1% annual fee paid quarterly on fund assets with no front-end or back-end commission.

Class K (R, etc.): Sometimes called "investor" class. Has no front-end or back-end fee, but charges a small fee of 0.25% - 0.5% per year.

Mutual funds that do not charge the extra fee or commission are called "no-load" funds. There is much debate over whether load or no-load funds offer the best returns. The answer is not as cut and dry as it seems. For example, if you constantly review the fund performances over 1 year, 3 years, 5 years or 10 years, the funds at the top include both load and no-load. There is much more to choosing funds than load or no-load categories. Sometimes "cost" does not mean "cost". What do we mean? For example, some money managers or advisors push the concept of only using no-load funds, but then charge a 1% annual fee to manage the no-load funds. This is precisely the same "cost" as using a Class C load fund which charges a 1% annual fee on assets. Another consideration is that often times the financial advisor who uses "load" funds does not charge fees for the other advice or the time to assist the client in other financial matters not related to the mutual funds. The point is to count the "costs" carefully before making a rash decision regarding load and no-load funds.

New Ideas for Fund Choices

There is a relatively new way to invest using the mutual fund strategy and this is called, Exchange Traded Funds (ETF's). These "funds" are developed by companies to simplify the diversification process and lower the annual fees. They invest in indexes, such as the S&P 500, the Russell 2000 or the NASDAQ 100, plus much more. Almost any index imaginable is represented, whether stocks or bonds. Maybe you want international corporate bonds or semiconductor stocks. They have it! Suppose you want biotech stock or the large cap value index. They have it!

Specific advantages of the ETF strategy include lower administrative fees and the ability to buy or sell at specific times during the day at specific prices. Mutual funds on the other hand, although purchased during the day, are actually traded at the end of the day after 4:00pm when the share prices are re-calculated. This means that you purchase the mutual funds not actually knowing the exact price of the purchase until the next day. ETF's function like a stock, so you know the price target and can purchase it when desired.

Another unique item related to ETF's is they are traded like a stock. There is no such thing as a load or no-load ETF. Commissions are charged exactly like a stock trade. You pay commission once when you buy and once at the point of sale.

A second new innovation is the area called "asset allocation" funds. The funds are actually a "fund of funds," based on the risk level of the investor. The choices range from conservative to moderate to aggressive. Instead of trying to pick the best fund, you pick your comfort zone regarding risk. The fund manager does the rest, spreading you into six to fifteen different funds, within the allocation fund. The advantage of course is broad diversification into many funds, plus professional asset allocation based on historical models. In a sense, it becomes risk management for the investor, which is what most people are concerned about anyway.

In summary, mutual funds should be considered by every investor as a way to enhance diversification and hire professional management for a minimal cost. The key is to take the necessary time to match the funds with your goals. Remember that past results or past fund performance does not guarantee future returns.

Notes

"An investor needs to do very few things right as long as he or she avoids big mistakes."
Warren Buffett

Chapter 9

STOCKS: Owning a Piece of the Action

One of the most common securities that investors own is the common stock. Stocks are sometimes called "equities" for a reason, because a stock is a form of direct ownership in a business or corporation. If an investor owns 100 shares of a company, they are an owner (in part) and have an equity stake in the business.

A second reason the stock ownership is popular among investors is the highly emotional attraction of owning stocks. Stocks, unlike most investments, are usually instantaneous in response to the market and other variables such as the economy and politics. Anyone can look on a computer via the Internet and find almost an immediate value on the share price or at worst a twenty minute delay price. Like a fighter pilot with a radar screen, the investor can "lock in" on a stock, pull the trigger, and a minute later, buy or sell the stock. There is an emotional rush for an investor with that kind of power.

When Do I Sell?

Here in lies the danger too. Sometimes investors get emotionally attached to the minute-by-minute swings in the stock market. There can be an addiction factor that can rob the investor of the potential joy and fulfillment of long term investment returns. The "Day Trading" mentality is only for the aggressive investor with a River Boat Gambler mentality. We do not recommend it.

The owner of equities holds a unique position in the investment community. For instance, the stock holder has the privilege of voting with the other stock holders on certain important company decisions. Ownership does have its privileges! Occasionally the stock holder receives a proxy in the mail to vote on certain items such as choosing a board member or changing a corporate policy. Annual reports are sent to the stock holder, giving the equity owner access to detailed financial information.

There are two very difficult decisions regarding stock ownership: when to buy and when to sell. Most veteran stock owners agree that the most anguishing decision of the two is when to sell. Emotion and stress runs high whether selling a stock that is up and very profitable or a stock that is down and money has been lost. Whether buying or selling a stock, one thing is a given: one person is selling the stock for his good reasons to another person who is purchasing the exact same stock for his own set of reasons. In every stock trade, one sells to someone who buys and one buys from someone who wants to sell. It's a "zero sum" game because each company has a finite number of shares. Unlike open-ended mutual funds, which can keep adding new shares as new money comes in, the stock of a company has an exact number of shares in the market (a company can float a new offering of shares to raise more money, but this dilutes the ownership of the current shareholders).

100

Whether purchasing or selling, there are several variables that effect the valuation and the future potential or demise of a stock. If you research the stock market, there are also hundreds of strategies and formulas that people use and swear-by on trading stock shares. For this book, we are going to review the most basic and easy to understand "variables" to use in stock trading as well as the two most basic strategies that have proved successful over the long term.

As mentioned earlier, each corporation has a finite number of shares. Each stock market around the world has a finite number of companies that they trade. For example, there are approximately 2,800 traded company stocks on the New York Stock Exchange and 3,340 stocks on the NASDAQ market, the two largest and most active markets in the world. Each day an investor can calculate the exact value that the markets believe a company is worth. For example, if a company has 100 million shares and the stock price closes that day at $20.00 per share, "Wall Street" says the company is worth 100,000,000 x $20.00 = $2 Billion. Even though this is a large number in the big business world, this is a rather small company. This value is called the "Market Cap" a shortened term for market capitalization. Professional investors have categorized a company's size:

> Large-cap = $10 Billion plus
> Mid-cap = $2 to $10 Billion
> Small-cap = $500 Million to $2 Billion
> Micro-cap = less than $500 Million

Large companies can generate large cash flows and have tens of thousands of employees in dozens of countries. Small caps can be nimble and can adjust more quickly to economic and market changes. More often than not, therefore, small caps have better growth opportunities than large companies, coming out of a recession, because they can adjust their business more quickly. Conservative investors may feel more comfortable owning very large companies because they are perceived as being more stable and more often than not, pay a cash dividend.

The market cap or valuation of a stock is a very important variable to investors, particularly to "value" investors. Two basic strategies of investors for years have been the "value" style and the "growth" style. Both styles or strategies have been successful over the decades, but usually not simultaneously. The late 90's saw the growth style out-perform the value style, while the early 2000's favored the value strategy over the growth strategy. What is the difference between these two successful strategies?

Value investors are looking for a "good deal", a stock "on the down", "cheap" or selling at a discount. A discount from what you may ask? A discount from the actual value of the company; the intrinsic value. Figuring the actual intrinsic value of a company is easier said than done. Assets are listed in the annual report along with debt, sales revenue, net income, etc. But there is more to the equation however, because no one can predict the future or when a company will rebound, cave in or excel. But value investors will methodically match up the value perceived on Wall Street (# of shares x $ per share) with their calculated intrinsic value. If the stock market value is significantly lower than the intrinsic value, the value investor will buy. When the market valuation goes significantly above the intrinsic value (hopefully), the investor will sell.

On the other hand, the "growth" investor is not necessarily concerned with the market value verses the intrinsic value of a business. They look at growth of earnings and sales. If the sales and earnings growth are accelerating, the growth investor will purchase the stock. Why? The reason is because high growth usually translates directly into stock price growth. Once the growth of earnings decelerates, the growth investor will usually sell the stock, regardless of the value of the company, whether stock market value or intrinsic value.

We recommend owning both value stocks and growth stocks in the same portfolio. Why? The reason is because both strategies have proven successful over the years and because the strategies go in and out of favor often in opposite directions.

Other methods are used to judge whether a stock is a good buy or a stock should be sold, such as looking at something called the P/E ratio. The P/E ratio is a simple mathematic equation where the numerator (P) is the "price per share" and the denominator (E) is the "earnings per share". So P/E is the price per share divided by the earnings per share. For example, if a stock is selling at $100/share and the company is earning $5/share, then the P/E ratio is $100 / $5 = 20. The P/E ratio is then used as a valuation in comparison to other stock's P/E ratios. For example, if you are debating the purchase of a restaurant stock, it may be helpful to compare the P/E's of all restaurant stocks or with the historic P/E ratio of that particular company. Also, it may be helpful to know that the P/E ratio of all stocks over the decades range around 15 to 16. This could be helpful if you discover a good quality company with sound financials with a P/E of only 8, which may tell you that the price of the stock is lower than it should be, motivating you to buy. But like all variables, there is another possible explanation; the company's business may be way down and thus a low P/E ratio. Using the P/E can be helpful, but be sure to remember how fractions work: there is a numerator and a denominator.

A second variable to keep an eye on is the amount of debt a company has accumulated. This is important to protect the investor on the down side. Suppose a company's business begins to go bad and the earnings go negative. If the company's debt is too great, the interest payments on the debt could eat up all of the profits, which are limited. Worst case the excessive debt could drag the company into bankruptcy. The stock price could take a severe down swing. On the other hand, if a company has millions of dollars in cash and securities with no debt on the books, this company can most likely survive a severe downturn in the economy or the business. If the stock price drops accordingly, the value investor would surely see an opportunity to buy.

Researching a company stock has become much easier over the last few years. The Internet has greatly enhanced the ability to review the historical prices and charts of most traded stocks. Analyst reviews, financial balance sheets and recent important news are now easily accessible.

Many investors either do not have the time to do research or they simply do not care to do the research. Fortunately, there are alternatives for these investors. The most common alternative are mutual funds which offer professional management, diversification and the ability to choose what type of stocks to hold based upon the category of the mutual fund.

A second method of stock investing using a professional would be the use of a money manager. A money manager is hired, usually for a fee such as 1% annually, to manage your portfolio of stocks and/or bonds. You delegate to the manager or a committee, through a limited power of attorney, to buy and sell inside of your account. The manager must keep you and all of their clients informed in regards to buys, sells and all activities in the account. Taxes are managed more easily with individual stock ownership than with mutual funds, which must declare dividends and capital gains annually, if they exist.

There is a misconception in regards to stock investing. Most investors would say that bonds, with their interest payments, are the safest and best method of generating income from assets. Not necessarily true! Stocks have interesting possibilities for the investor looking for income. Many stocks pay quarterly dividends, and cash dividends are an important part of the overall return.

Another special type of company stock must by law share dividends with investors. These stocks are called REITS (Real Estate Investment Trusts). By law a REIT does not pay corporate income taxes, but in turn must payout in dividends to investors -- 90% of their earnings. Because of the earnings from real estate (which is typically income producing), REITS tend to pay excellent dividends to investors.

Some investors like dividend paying stocks but do not need the current income. There is an option to reinvest the dividends into new shares of the same stock. This strategy is called a dividend reinvestment plan or DRIP's. Of course you will pay taxes on the dividends, but over the long term, your number of stock shares will increase on a regular basis.

A second, sometimes overlooked way that stocks can provide income is through selling appreciated stocks. Long term capital gains taxes (held for at least 12 months) were reduced in 2003 to 15% Federal, the same tax as on stock dividends. Congress tends to change the capital gains tax every few years, but selling highly appreciated stocks and paying taxes can sometimes give the investor a better after tax income than paying income taxes on bond and CD interest. For example, if you purchased a stock 12 months ago for $2,000 and sell it today for $3,000, you have a $1,000 long term gain. After paying taxes of 15% = $150, you have generated $850 of income (assuming no state tax). On the other hand, it could take years to accumulate $850 cash, after taxes, on a $3,000 bond or CD investment.

Speaking of taxes and the law, there is a clever strategy to "harvest" taxes on a stock that unfortunately may have tanked on you. It is called a "wash sale". The IRS code allows an investor to sell a "loser" stock and after waiting at least 31 days, the same stock can be repurchased in that account. Why would an investor do such a thing? Because the investor can take the capital loss, deduct it from their income and claim the loss against income taxes. Under current law, $3,000 of capital losses is allowed each year even after matching up your capital losses against capital gains. If your losses exceed your gains by even more than $3,000 in any given year, you are allowed to carry forward any remaining losses in future years. The risk in executing a wash sale is that before the 31st day passes, the sold stock could rebound in price and could cost you more to purchase. Of course you are not obligated to purchase that stock again. Incidentally there is some cost in doing a wash sale which includes two commissions paid, one at the sale and one at the time of repurchase.

One of the most effective ways to leverage your gifting to a charity or a church is by using highly appreciated stocks. Instead of writing a check, why not give the stock? You save the capital gains tax by giving the stock away, while the church or charity can sell the stock tax free. Your "cost" verses your tax write-off for the charitable gift can offer tremendous financial advantages. Note the following example:

Purchase 100 shares @ $10/share = $1,000
Current Value @ $25/share = $2,500
Capital Gain of $15/share = $1,500

SELLING	GIVING
$1,500 Gain	$2,500 Gift
x 22% Tax Bracket* (Capital Gains)	x 30% Tax Bracket (Income)
$ 330 Taxes Due	$ 750 Taxes Saved

*15% Federal; 7% State

For the long term investor who likes the idea of growth potential, good quality portfolio of stocks have been hard to beat.

When compared to many other investment tools such as real estate, bonds, CD's, cash, etc., stocks outperform in almost any 5, 10, 25 or 100 year time period.

With that said, stocks carry with them a volatility factor that can be severe. Stocks have to be watched carefully and handled with care, but the rewards can truly be satisfying. Patience is the virtue that all stock investors must maintain.

"You can't produce a baby in one month by getting nine women pregnant."
Warren Buffett

Notes

"A billion here, a billion there, pretty soon it
adds up to real money."
Senator Everett Dirksen

Chapter 10

BONDS

Often we speak to people in a seminar environment. Sometimes when we review diversification of a portfolio, we distinguish the difference between stocks and bonds by defining them in their basic form. Inevitably, after the seminar meeting someone will come up and say, "Thank you for that. I never knew the difference between a stock and a bond until tonight."

What Is a Bond?

A bond is *essentially* a loan. When I purchase a bond, I am loaning my money to someone and that someone is paying interest to me for the use of my money. Typically, bonds pay interest semi-annually. Who borrows the money? The U.S. government is the largest borrower, but also corporations, cities, counties and even churches borrow money by floating their bonds to investors.

Like any loan, a bond has a maturity date. For instance, your state government may float a 10-year bond @ 4%

interest. That means that if you purchase $10,000 worth of bonds on the first day it is available, you will receive 4% annual interest or $400 per year, but it will be paid to you $200 every six months. If you hold the bond for the 10 full years, you will receive your $10,000 back and the loan is completed and the bond turns into cash.

Types of Bonds

There are many types of bonds. Government bonds are very common and are interesting because they have certain tax benefits:

U.S. Government Bonds: State tax-free on interest earned

Municipal Bonds (State, City, etc.): Federal tax-free on interest earned

Municipal bonds are typically any type of government bonds other than federal, but can also be local bonds used to fund hospitals, airports, sewer systems, etc.

Corporate bonds are often used by businesses to borrow money. Instead of going to the banks, a corporation can issue a bond and in effect borrow money from hundreds of investors.

High yield bonds, sometimes called "junk bonds", offer higher interest rates but also offer more risk to investors because the company may have a weaker financial status or be a new company with little history of success.

Bond Ratings

The good news for investors is that bonds are rated by independent rating services based upon the bond backers' financial viability. The ratings go from "AAA", the best rating, to "C", the lowest rating. Investment grade bonds, the more "secure" variety, are rated from "AAA" to "BBB". Any bond rated below "BBB" is usually rendered higher risk and falls into the high yield or junk bond arena.

The rating of the bond is one of the several variables that affect the return yield. A commonly misunderstood concept is in play here. The financially safer the issuer of a bond, the higher grading it receives. With the higher rating comes a lower yield return. Conversely, the lower the rating, the higher the yield return. As in any investment, the investor is rewarded for taking more risk, but with that risk comes a greater possibility of a loss.

Bond Mutual Funds

Many investors today enjoy or prefer the benefits of owning securities in a mutual fund to provide increased diversification and professional management. Like individual bonds, there are many different types of bond funds. There are U.S. government, foreign government, municipal, corporate, and high yield (junk) bond funds. There are even highly diversified funds that include all of the above in one fund. Because mutual funds are highly scrutinized and are required to reveal voluminous information, investors can quickly find the important bond parameters such as the average rating and maturity of all the bonds held by the fund. Of course the fund manager is constantly evaluating his or her portfolio, buying and selling, and repositioning to make adjustments to the variables in the market. Note that bond interest can be reinvested into the bond fund rather than taking the interest in cash as individual bond holders must do.

There is one other key difference in owning individual bonds verses owning bond mutual funds. The difference is how often the interest is paid to the investor. Individual bonds pay interest semi-annually, but mutual funds pay monthly. This is very important to investors who have a goal of cash flow. Generally it is easier to budget one's cash flow monthly than semi-annually. Therefore, for that particular investor the bond mutual fund is perhaps the best choice.

Tax laws are similar for bond funds and individual bonds. U.S. government bond fund's interest is not taxed by your state government tax code. Municipal bond fund's interest is not taxed by the federal tax code, however, remember that municipal bond funds usually hold bonds from a number of different states. If the investor wants to save taxes both federally and state, they need to find a state-specific mutual fund that only owns municipal bonds from their state. Keep in mind that like all mutual funds, the IRS requires funds to declare all dividends and capital gains annually. This simply means that if the fund manager trades bonds during the year and if there are any capital gains, taxes will be due on the investor's tax returns. If the investor owns individual bonds, the capital gains or losses on a bond sale, are controlled by the investor.

Risks

Bonds have unique risks as compared to other investments. Most investments do not have a set date of maturity, so one of the risks is that it has a definite ending date. Why is that a risk? Because if you owned an old bond that was paying high interest, tax-free, you would want to keep that bond potentially forever, but that bond will end absolutely on the date of maturity.

A second misunderstood risk unique to bonds is interest rate risk. Think of this risk as a seesaw. When interest rates go up, bond prices go down. When interest rates go down, bond prices go up.

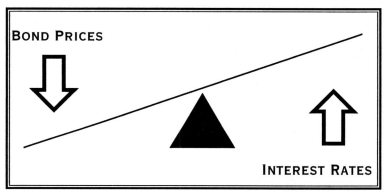

Bond prices and interest rates are inversely related—like a see-saw!

Why is the risk a reality? Think of it this way. Let's say that two years ago I purchased a 10-year $10,000 bond at par (value of bond without a discount or premium; ex. $10,000 bond at par is worth $10,000), and it has a coupon or interest rate of 6%. So I have been collecting $600 in interest annually. But now two years later, the prevailing interest rates paid on new bonds of similar maturity and rating is 7%. If you are a new investor looking to purchase a bond, which one would you prefer? My bond paying 6% interest or the new bonds paying 7% interest? Of course you would pick the 7% bond. If I wanted you to buy my bond I could entice you in one way only – I could lower the price (discount)! If I could lower my sales price enough to approximate your desired return of 7% like the new bonds, you might purchase it from me. When rates rise, bond prices fall, whether it is on individual bonds or bonds in a mutual fund.

A third risk that exists on most fixed income securities such as bonds is inflation risk. Inflation has averaged about

3% annually for the last 50 years. This can be a serious risk if you hold a long-term bond to maturity. Suppose you bought a $10,000 ten-year bond at par value paying 6% interest and you hold it for the full ten-year term. On the maturity date you would receive your $10,000 back. But remember, your $10,000 is your "old" $10,000. If inflation had averaged 3% per year, you would have "lost" a significant amount of purchasing power. That means what cost you $10,000 ten-years ago now costs you $13,440. To put it another way, your principal never grows. You may have enjoyed the interest return, but your principal actually loses to inflation over time.

A fourth risk is an early call date by whoever issues the bond. "Calling" the bond means its issuer can liquidate the bond on a certain date at a certain price. Take the previous example of the ten-year $10,000 bond. If the issuer has a call date four years from the issue date at par value, this means if prevailing interest rates have fallen significantly enough, the issuer, for good business reasons, may choose to call the bond. Later, if desired, they could re-issue new bonds at the lower prevailing interest rate. But your original bond has disappeared and turned into cash when it was called.

Rewards of Owning Bonds

Bonds add value to any portfolio. Bonds sometimes move in opposite directions to stocks, so bonds help balance and stabilize your portfolio. Recent history bares this out. During the late 90's the stock market had one of its greatest run-ups in history, while bonds languished with mediocre returns. Then from early 2000 through October 2002, stocks had their greatest three-year drop off since 1939- 1941, while bond returns were outstanding, leading all sectors.

A second advantage of bonds is their production of income on a regular basis. If one goal for the investor is income, the bonds generally pay as good or better rates than other fixed income investments such as CD's or money markets. Taxes can be reduced by purchasing various types of government or municipal bonds. CD's are always taxable on both state and federal tax returns. Generally, bonds are considered more conservative overall than stocks. Many people increase bond holdings as they near retirement. However, because of their lack of growth potential, retirees should always seek balance in their portfolios.

Unique Bonds

There are certain types of bonds that are very unique. As always, these bond types must match up with your goals. Sometimes the investor does not want immediate income from a bond. To resolve that issue, the investor can purchase a zero coupon bond. This type of bond is purchased at a discount of the face value, exactly the same way as another unique type of bond, the Savings Bond issued by the U.S. government. For example, a person could purchase a 10-year zero coupon bond paying 7.2% interest per year to pay for their 8 year old's freshman year of college ten years later. If the bond face value were $20,000, the cost of the bond would be $10,000. As the interest accrues over the years with no payment to the investor, the bond can be sold at anytime with credit for the accrued interest before it matures. The interest is taxable at the time of sale or at maturity. Incidentally, U.S. savings bond interest can be tax exempted if the proceeds are used for college education purposes.

Finally, another unique type of bond is called a convertible bond. The word "convertible" means that at a point in time the bond can be converted to the issuing company's common stock. The rate of conversion or the price per share of stock is pre-set from the beginning. The interest rate on this bond is usually lower than comparable corporate bonds, but the potential upside is attractive to some investors who want broad diversification combining income and growth.

Conclusion

Always consider bonds as a percentage of any investment portfolio for better balance and diversification. Consider tax planning to be part of your selection process when choosing bonds. Always keep bonds near the top of your list when income and cash flow are part of your near term goals.

Notes

_____

_____

_____

_____

_____

_____

_____

_____

_____

_____

_____

_____

_____

_____

"The highest use of capital is not to make more money, but to make money do more for the betterment of life."
(Henry Ford)

*"If you can count your money, you don't
have a billion dollars."*
J. Paul Getty

Chapter 11

Real Estate: Building Your Portfolio from the Ground Up

Over the last one hundred years a good case could be made that the real estate returns are neck and neck with the stock market. The old adage is true, "they are not making any more of it." Whenever there is a limited supply of anything along with a growing demand, prices and values are going to rise. Another old adage is also true about real estate and its value, "location, location, location." Clearly there is a huge difference in value between beachfront property and desert dunes forty miles from the nearest city. In both cases the product is sand, but the location of the sand makes all the difference in the world.

Real estate is definitely an attractive area to invest, but it carries with it some limitations. One limitation is the inherent lack of liquidity. In other words, real estate is a tangible asset, a hard asset, but not easily transferable. You can see it, walk on it and drill holes in it, but it is not liquid! The market however, has answered this limitation with a special stock called a real estate investment trust or REIT. We will discuss REIT's later. A second limitation for real estate is the fact that it is not usually sold in small pieces like a share of stock. Real estate is sold in large chunks and therefore more money is usually involved in the investment.

The Founding Fathers knew when creating our constitution that one of the foundational rights of a free and democratic republic was the right to own property.

By creating and encouraging personal property ownership and rights to protection, the Founding Fathers placed a value on real estate.

To insure that this constitutional right was encouraged, certain tax benefits have been created for owners of real estate.

Tax savings often are a key element in making real estate an attractive investment. Often when a young married couple comes to my office for advice, I suggest they put purchasing a house near the top of their goals list. Why? A double benefit exists. First, the taxes saved are significant when owning property verses renting a property. The residence offers two income tax deductions: the interest on the mortgage and the real estate taxes imposed by the city and county. Second there is a great likelihood that the house will increase in value over time creating equity or increased value in the investment. The house after all is an investment. The tax savings can be the difference in affording to own property and not affording to own property.

Example (Two bedroom apartment):

Renting costs	= $800/month
Owning costs	= $900/month

(6%, 30-year loan, $150,000 mortgage)

At first glance, the cost of owning looks greater than the cost of renting. Since mortgages are amortized in such a way that the first few years of payments are mostly interest and the last few years are mostly principal, the tax write-offs are large in the early years. Add to this the tax deduction for the real estate taxes and the "cost" to own is lower than the "cost" to rent. Suppose our couple is in the 30% state and federal income tax bracket. Take a second look at the numbers.

Mortgage Interest plus real estate taxes	= $800/month (of the $900/month payment)
Tax bracket	x 30%
Tax savings	= $240/month
Owning costs (gross)	= $900/month (mortgage payment)
Adjustment for tax savings	= $240/month
Owning costs (net)	= $660/month

Not only is owning property less expensive potentially than renting, but the couple can decrease their income tax withholding at work to increase their cash flow, knowing that $240 per month in taxes are being saved monthly. The adjustment to their salary will easily offset the increase payment of $900 per month for the mortgage verses the smaller $800 per month rental payment.

What about investment real estate other than the home? There are many varieties to choose from including owning a second home. Congress allows the same mortgage interest and real estate tax deductions for a second home, just as they do for the first home, up to a ceiling of $100,000 per year. Many people dream of owning a vacation get-away at the beach, lake or mountains. Again, the tax laws for real estate make the possibility more attractive and more affordable.

A second choice would be to own a rental property. The rental property could be either residential or commercial. The commercial property could vary from warehouses to retail stores to office buildings. Residential rental property could vary from condos to apartments to single family dwellings.

Rental property offers similar tax benefits such as owning your residence with two exceptions. One exception is that all expenses related to running a rental property are also tax deductible. Items included are things such as advertising, repairs, improvements and mileage to and fro regarding the property. However, do not forget that the offset to these write-offs is that the rental income is income taxable. The equity growth is not taxed over the years until a property sale is made. At that point the capital gains tax applies. Rental property has a second exception that allows additional tax benefits. It is called depreciation. The IRS assumes the property will deteriorate over time and improvements will be made, or else the building will become less valuable. The government has various depreciation tables. Let's assume a property can be depreciated over 30 years and the value is $100,000.00. By dividing the value by the number of depreciation years, the owner can deduct $3,333.00 annually off the income, reducing taxes. At sale however, the IRS requires the owner to recapture the depreciation and pay capital gains taxes. In our example, if the owner held the property 10 years, he would have deducted $33,333.00 (10 x $3,333). All $33,333.00 would be "recaptured" at the sale of the property and would be subject to capital gains taxes. Under current law however, the Federal capital gains tax is less than most people's income tax, so owing rental property remains a tax advantage.

Raw land is another way to invest in real estate. This area usually involves more risk and speculation. For one thing, owning raw land does not generate income. Meantime, the investor would have to pay real estate taxes on the property. The investor must be patient as well because raw land is often sitting dormant until a developer or someone really wants the property. Raw land however, can be a very lucrative investment especially if it is located in an area of growth. Sometimes the appreciation can be dramatic. Raw land investing therefore tends to be feast or famine, and not for the faint of heart, nor for one that cannot afford the risk.

Earlier we mentioned that the lack of liquidity sometimes is a barrier to investors. The REIT or real estate investment trust could be the answer. The REIT is actually a stock company that owns real estate or real estate related entities. The company's stock trades just like any other stock on the stock market. Just as there are various types of real estate, there are various types of REIT stocks. Take your pick; the options range from shopping centers to apartments to condo's or even mortgage REIT's. A unique thing about the earnings of a REIT company involves how the earnings are used. By law the REIT must pay to the stock holders 90% of its earnings. In exchange for this they do not pay corporate taxes. This law creates dividends for the investor and they are usually quite strong as compared to normal common stock dividends. The investor then has some of the same advantages of owning real estate outright: income plus potential equity growth with the added benefit of having instant liquidity thanks to the stock exchange.

We should mention that there are also unlisted REIT's available to investors. Several companies have created REIT's purposely designed not to be listed until a future time on the stock market (therefore, for a while, not very liquid). Before jumping to any conclusions, consider that not being listed can be a plus when the stock market is taking an extended drop or is extremely volatile. Conceptually the unlisted REIT will pay a competitive dividend while waiting to become listed on the exchange, and is growing in equity similar to any other real estate. At the IPO (initial public offering), the stock price could potentially be set at a higher price than the original offering price, but also could be lower—a risk of the investment. Unusual investments like REIT's can be a very creative alternative for people with smaller amounts of cash to invest or who desire liquidity.

Real estate done properly should appreciate in value over time.

When the day comes to sell the property at a nice profit, capital gains taxes can become a barrier. There are several interesting strategies available for real estate investors that can reduce the tax impact of a real estate sale.

The first strategy, unique to real estate, is called the 1031 like-kind exchange, which allows an investor to exchange one type of real estate investment for another real estate investment (Figure 11.1). In effect, this exchange transfers the cost basis (original cost) from property #1 to property #2, thus deferring the capital gains to the next property. No capital gains taxes are paid because of the exchange. Current rules require the target property to be identified within 45 days from the sale of property #1, with a closing due no later than 180 days after sale. Multiple exchanges are allowed over the years if necessary. One key case in which the 1031 exchange is very useful is when an elderly investor owns highly appreciated raw land but has low income and poor cash flow. By exchanging raw land for a rental property with nice cash flow, the owners can sell the property, pay no capital gains taxes and dramatically increase their cash flow. Remember however, that the cost basis of any real estate investment property jumps up to current market value, at the death of the owner. By allowing the cost basis to increase to the current market value at the death of the owner, the beneficiaries can sell the property later with little or no capital gains tax.

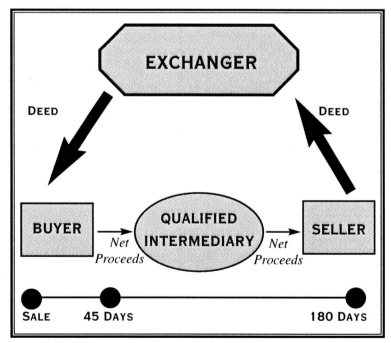

Figure 11.1. *Typical 1031 Tax-Deferred Exchange*

A second strategy that fits nicely for highly appreciated real estate is discussed in the Estate Planning and Trust chapter. Briefly, the highly appreciated real estate asset is placed in a Charitable Remainder Trust and then sold. Capital gains taxes are avoided and the trust, by design, pays an income stream to the donors until the death of the donor (or donors if married) or family members. In addition the trust removes the real estate from the estate, avoiding any future estate taxes. A partial income tax deduction is also created by the contribution to the trust. At the death of the donors the remaining trust assets are given to a designated charity, church or school. Whenever a trust strategy is used to transfer assets, be sure to have competent attorneys and a financial planner to assist with the process.

Real estate has many unique benefits, investment-wise and tax-wise. Real estate should be in every investor's asset allocation plan. Diversification matters greatly in the investment world and we recommend between 10% and 20% real estate holdings. The Wall Street version of diversification is usually defined as stocks, bonds and cash. But research has indicated that the addition of real estate can potentially improve returns while reducing volatility. Real estate makes sense for every investor.

Notes

_____

_____

_____

_____

_____

_____

_____

_____

_____

_____

_____

_____

_____

"Every time you spend money, you're casting a vote for the kind of world you want."
(Anna Lappe)

*"The trick is to make sure you don't die
waiting for prosperity to come."*
Lee Iacocca

Chapter 12

Annuities: Tax-Deferred Plus More

Of all the possible investment vehicles available for investors, the annuity has gone through the largest evolution of change over the last decade. Years ago, annuities were rather boring investments that mainly attracted conservative people because of their safety and tax deferred qualities. The annuities of today however, are not your grandmother's annuity!

Annuities remind some people of IRA's or retirement plans. As a matter of fact, the annuity possesses some of the same IRS rules as IRA plans. Namely, the annuity's assets grow tax deferred and if you withdraw the assets before age 59.5, there is a 10% tax penalty. Clearly then, annuities are designed for long term growth and focuses on the retirement years, after 59.5.

In other ways however, the annuity possesses some traits that are unique unto itself. For example, an annuity can be used for a regular account with after tax money (called a "non-qualified" plan) or for an IRA (or retirement plan) with pretax or non-taxed money (called a "qualified" plan). Annuities funded with non-qualified money are however, not required to distribute a required minimum distribution (RMD) at age 70.5 like IRA and other retirement plans.

Basically, annuities can be divided into two different categories. The first type is also the oldest type and is called a fixed annuity. Fixed annuities are "fixed" into only one type of investment that pays an interest rate, usually guaranteed for one year. Each year the annuity company adjusts the interest rates according to the current market rates. More often than not, the annuity company will entice investors with a higher interest rate than provided by current market rates. Keep in mind that this higher initial rate usually lasts only 12 months and then will be adjusted back down to current market rates.

Tax Deferred Growth

One unique trait of a fixed annuity is that you can purchase fixed rates for a set number of years. The longer the holding period, the higher the interest rate will be. For example, a fixed annuity may pay you 4% annually for one year, 5% for three years and 6% for five years. If you pull the money out early, before the required holding period, there is a severe penalty. However, if you have cash set aside for the long haul and want conservation with guarantees; a long term fixed annuity may fit the bill. These annuities are least attractive when prevailing interest rates are low and most attractive when rates are high. The lure of tax-deferred growth is always attractive regardless of the interest rates.

A second type of annuity that has become very popular in recent years is called the variable annuity. The word "variable" means various investments which you can ultimately choose will have returns that are variable. Typically these investments are in funds that mimic mutual funds, managed by various mutual fund companies. This annuity looks consequently like a large 401(K) plan with an array of mutual fund choices, but it is not a 401(K) plan. The beauty of the variable annuity is that it allows the investor to have access to a very large asset allocation pool, giving the person an opportunity to maximize the diversification of assets, to customize the plan for risk tolerance and potential growth. Assets can be repositioned at will without a fee to adjust to market changes or risk adjustments. Of course the variable annuity retains all the tax-deferred benefits.

During the '90's the stock market grew rapidly and then was followed by the longest market downturn (2000-2002) since the beginning of World War II.

With those volatile amazing market runs, both positive and negative, annuity companies have added many enhancements to make annuities more attractive to investors.

There are too many to mention here, but we will highlight the most common and beneficial.

First, there is the enhanced death benefit. Originally, the annuity companies guaranteed the initial premium so that if the annuity owner died while the market was down, the beneficiary still received the original investment. Later the companies started "ratcheting" the death benefit annually, meaning the death benefit is adjusted on the annual anniversary date if the annuities asset value is higher than the year before. This meant even more safety for the beneficiaries if the market was down when the owner died. Most people never realized how important this benefit would be until it happened to annuity owners in the real world. Many people had annuity values run dramatically higher in the late '90's. What if unfortunately they died in 2002 or 2003, after the severe downfall of stocks from their all-time highs? For example, an investor started a variable annuity with $50,000 in 1995 and by year 2000 the value had reached $100,000. After the three year down cycle, the asset value dropped to $75,000 and the annuity owner died in early 2003. Because of the enhanced death benefit, the beneficiary received the full $100,000, not the current market value of $75,000.

A second interesting annuity enhancement is the initial bonus of asset value, usually 4% or even 5%. If you invest $20,000 into a bonus annuity, your asset value is immediately $21,000. Why did the companies do this? Because annuities are designed for the long term, there are usually surrender charges if you pull the money out early from the annuity. Typically the surrender fees decline each year. For example, an annuity may have a scale starting at 7% surrender charge in year one, 6% in year two, declining 1% annually down to 0% in the seventh year! Annuities today offer many variations of surrender charges. Carefully check the surrender charges of the annuity *before* investing. Now, most companies even have annuities with zero surrender charges. The bonus annuity was created, therefore, to offset surrender charges from old annuities that investors wished to vacate. The new bonus annuity simply offsets the surrender charge on the old annuity. The good news is that the bonus annuity is not automatically tied to an old annuity, so any investor can open a bonus annuity and receive the bonus with brand new money.

Speaking of fees, all of the enhancements, "bells and whistles," come with some additional fees. Surprised? You should not be because nothing worthwhile in life comes free. All of the enhancements and guarantees have their "costs" which are usually fractional or less than 1% per year. For example, a non-enhanced annuity may cost 1.8% annually to administer, where a "fully enhanced" annuity could cost 3.1% annually. Check the fine print on how the enhancement will add to your cost. Also ask your advisor for information.

A more recent enhancement is the guarantee on growth of principle. These are usually called "living benefits" as compared to death benefits. In other words, can an investor in stock and bond mutual funds have their cake and eat it too? Apparently yes! While invested in the market, the annuities will deliver a guarantee of 5%, 6% or even 7% annual net return. Usually the guarantee lasts until assets double or triple. The fee is usually 0.5% - 0.8% annually. There is typically a restriction on the ultimate withdrawal if you chose to generate returns with guarantees. You must "annuitize" the account upon withdrawing the money.

"Annuitization" is another unique strategy of annuities. It has to do with how an investor withdraws money from the annuity. Let's assume you invested in a non-qualified annuity with $50,000. Years later as you enter retirement, assets had grown to $100,000. If you pulled money out, the IRS says, "No problem," but you will have to pull out the "growth" first (which has grown tax-deferred). This means it is 100% taxable. Once the growth money is fully withdrawn, then the after tax money is withdrawn tax free. You can choose however, to "annuitize" your annuity. Your choices can include either a certain number of years or a certain amount until the money runs out or over your lifetime until death. If you annuitize, the whole asset is used to deliver the money, which reduces taxes. In our example, there is $50,000 which has already been taxed and another $50,000 that has never been taxed. The income stream will be 50% tax free based on the ratio of taxed and non-taxed money. It is simple math:

$50,000 tax-deferred / $100,000 total value = 50% taxable income

Annuities have been criticized in the media for having excessively high fees. Other criticism comes from critics who cannot rationalize opening a tax deferred IRA by using a tax deferred annuity. Like most critics, they tend to over-generalize. In financial planning there are so many variables that making a generalized blanket statement or opinion is not wise. The truth is that for the extra fees, something of value is received. Honest financial advisors will tell you the benefits and costs of any investment, including annuities. The fact is that very few investment vehicles exist that have guarantees attached. Annuities happen to be one of them. So if a client enters my office and states that they want to try to get a competitive market return but want some guarantees either on the investment growth or for the beneficiary, then annuities will be one of the items to review and discuss. Annuities are appropriate for certain clients with certain goals, so do not believe all the negative hype in the media.

Notes

"Certainly there are things in life that money
can t buy, but it's very funny—
Did you ever try buying them without money?"
(Ogden Nash)

*"Why insure everything you own for what it's worth except
your life, your most important asset?
Each man is a money making machine and should be
insured for what he is worth."*
Ben Feldman

Chapter 13

Insurance: Managing Risk

Insurance is a centuries old solution to managing risk. The concept of insurance is actually quite simple. The theory is that since each person in a group is exposed to certain risks, the group as a whole could protect the individuals in the group by sharing the risk among them.

For example, take homeowners insurance. If I own a $200,000 house and still owe $100,000 on my mortgage, I have a large financial exposure. If my house burned to the ground, not only do I lose my home and belongings, but I have to figure a way to rebuild my house and pay off the $100,000 loan. A financial disaster and an emotional disaster are always looming. An excellent solution would be if thousands of fellow homeowners each contributed, say $500 per year into a pooled investment strategy, safe but growing, in order to create a safety net just incase several individuals are met with an unfortunate disaster. Three factors should exist to create the safety net: having enough people in the group, contributions coming into the pooled account regularly, and investments continuing to grow.

Then each individual can rely on the safety net if ever needed. This is the concept of insurance: protecting the individual by participating with the larger group.

Over the years, the insurance industry has developed to the point where almost anything that has a risk of loss can be insured. Athletes insure their bodies, their championship rings, their trophies, while governments insure their satellite launches. But for our discussion we will limit ourselves to the most common and necessary types of insurances: life, health, disability and long-term care.

Health & Disability Insurance

Health insurance is something that is covered almost all the time, in part or in full, by our employer. Companies view this benefit as a way to recruit quality employees and retain those employees. Many businesses also allow employees to cover their spouses and children. Because of the soaring costs of health care and hospitalization, even though the premiums (or payments) for health insurance seem high, most Americans are getting a pretty good deal. If you are self-employed, unemployed or work part time, you may not have health insurance. Many people do not realize that some companies specialize in individual health care policies. Shop around and you will find these companies through agents or on the Internet, rather than assuming you cannot afford health insurance.

During our working years another type of insurance is important, but often overlooked. This is disability insurance. Sometimes a business, especially if it is a large one, offers some type of short term or long-term disability insurance. If your employer does not offer it, or if you are self-employed, you should investigate disability insurance for your own benefit. A simple definition of disability insurance is "income replacement." When you purchase disability insurance you are purchasing "income replacement" for the future, incase you are disabled and can no longer work or make a living. The cost of your insurance depends on how much replacement income you are "buying" and for how long it will last. For example, if your income is $4,000 per month and you need $2,500 per month income for 5 years, due to a disability, you can apply for that amount of coverage. No insurance company will replace 100% of lost income. The maximum replacement income percentage is 67% of salary. This is to keep unethical people from abusing the insurance benefit. A further restriction is that a doctor must validate, in writing, that a disability has caused the patient to lose income because of the inability to perform their job (called "own occupation") and in some cases, any job. If your company pays the premiums and you are disabled, the income is taxable. If you pay for the premiums and are disabled, then income is tax free. Investigate disability insurance because losing your income is a recipe for financial disaster!

Once we finish our working careers and face retirement, we face a whole new set of health care issues and types of insurance. At 65 years old, each American is eligible to receive Medicare coverage. This discussion will be simplified to say that Medicare has a Part A and Part B which covers hospitalization and Doctors' care respectively. It costs money for the government to cover a percentage of these costs for retiree's, so each working person pays premiums from their paychecks into a government pool. Like any insurance in the health arena, not all the costs are covered. A misconception about Medicare is that 100% of health costs are covered during retirement. Not true! There are co-payments which mean each person must pay some of the health costs that Medicare does not cover.

On top of that co-payment, there are deductibles to pay which are 100% out of pocket costs before the Medicare payments kick into play. In addition, Medicare does not cover everything, such as the cost of pharmaceuticals. The insurance industry has created something called Medi-Gap insurance. By design this insurance fills the gap between our pocketbook and Medicare coverage. There are many types of policies, but the average person who is nearing age 65 must take the time to investigate the options of Medi-Gap insurance and the coverage that Medicare offers.

LTC

After retirement or even before retirement, there is another insurance that has similar characteristics to disability insurance. It is called long-term care insurance. Long-term care insurance (LTC) is similar to disability insurance in that the individual is purchasing an income stream for a debilitating health issue. LTC insurance provides an income stream of a certain amount of dollars per day needed for long-term care, whether nursing home, skilled nursing, adult day care or home health care. The average cost of a LTC facility is $145 per day. A second similarity to disability insurance is that the income stream is for a specific length of time, even up to lifetime. For example, a LTC policy can be purchased for a benefit of $125 per day for up to 5 years. As modern medicine and biotech pharmaceuticals lengthen our lives, long-term care is less and less an optional insurance but one of necessity. With the average care facility costing $40,000 to $50,000 annually, a long-term catastrophic illness can wipe out the estate of a family.

So what are the options?

1. Using personal assets. But how much and how long will personal assets last?

2. Accessing limited Medicare benefits. However, Medicare Part A pays no more than 100 days of inpatient care in a skilled nursing facility per benefit period. Days 1-20 Medicare pays 100%. Days 21-100 are only partially covered. Medicare is not the answer!

3. Qualifying for Medicaid welfare program. Medicaid is the government funded program with stringent financial eligibility requirements that must be met in order to receive benefits. If you decide to "spend down" your assets or if you are forced to, consider an asset test. As of January 2004, Medicaid has three categories of assets: non-countable, countable and inaccessible. To simplify, you must be in poverty, owning less than $2,000 in assets other than your home, car and personal belongings.

Also there is a 3 year "look back" provision on any transfers of assets. The government can come back and claim assets given away in the last 36 months! There are discussions that may make that a 5 year look back.

So again, back to my original question, "How do we protect our assets from a critical care need such as long term care?"

Well the better option is to buy long term care insurance. What is the best age to do this? There is no magic number here! We recommend you consider long term care insurance at least between ages 50-60. The cost of coverage is directly related to your age. Always consider lifetime coverage, inflation protection and whether or not skilled care and home healthcare are covered.

There are life insurance policies now that offer LTC benefits. See chart in Chapter 1 for details.

One of the questions I get from time to time is "Can I get life insurance if I have a health problem?" Well, these life insurance policies are typically done as second-to-die (insuring 2 lives) which is more cost effective than insuring only one life. If there is a healthy spouse, usually it is easier to get the policy written.

In addition to the life insurance strategy, there are now annuity companies that offer LTC riders on their annuities. I know of one company that even writes policies on seniors already in a nursing home. There are so many new and improved options concerning LTC insurance. Please ask a professional to give you information on all that is available to you. A financial planner is a good source of information; start there!

Life Insurance

The most common and recognizable type of insurance is life insurance. Life insurance pays a death benefit to the beneficiaries of the deceased. Over the years, life insurance has been used for even more solutions than simply protecting the family of the deceased. Corporations use life insurance to create special benefits for key employees and owners. People with a high net worth use life insurance to pay estate taxes and create estate liquidity for their heirs. But the most common use of life insurance is for the protection of a family. If a family bread winner dies, the family needs financial protection. "Family" is the key word here.

How much life insurance do I need?

Sometimes I am asked by single adults or young married couples without children if they need life insurance. In most cases my answer is "no." Why? Because life insurance is to protect the lifestyle of your heirs; in particular your younger heirs. Most singles have no heirs, unless there are children from a previous marriage, and most young married's have no children. With both spouses earning a salary, income loss will not destroy the life of the surviving spouse if one spouse should die "early." Once the young couple has children, then life insurance becomes important. If a parent dies prematurely or unexpectedly, the surviving family will be under emotional duress. If the loss of income is significant, there will be financial distress as well. This is what life insurance is for, to protect the beneficiaries from financial distress.

A common question is, "How much life insurance do I need?" The answer is not the same for everyone. A somewhat simplified way to estimate the amount needed for families are these steps:

1. Take the annual income for each working spouse and multiply by 75% (this is because after one spouse dies, the expenses of the family are reduced by approximately 25%).

2. For non-working spouses the death benefit should be approximately $200,000.

3. After completing step 1, take the number and divide by 6% (this is because the investment portfolio created from the lump sum death benefit should generate approximately 6% cash flow annually without undue risk over time.

4. The final number is approximately how much insurance needed by the working spouse.

5. Make any financial adjustments.

Example:
Dad earns $80,000 / year
Mom is a homemaker, works part time
Couple has two children, age 6 and 3
  Step 1: $80,000 x 75% = $60,000

  Step 2: Nonworking spouse = $200,000 life
                    insurance needed

  Step 3: $60,000 / 6% = $1,000,000 life insurance
                    needed for working spouse

At first glance this example seems like too much insurance is needed. Remember first of all, that this is the ideal case. Second, almost all businesses offer corporate group life insurance which means less insurance is needed from our personal policy. Third, we make adjustments according to needs. For instance, if the sample couple's children were 21 and 18 years old with college expenses already covered, the couple would not need nearly as much protection from life insurance.

There is an old saying that no one ever died with too much life insurance.

As I have sat across from clients who have lost a spouse through death, I can attest to the fact that too much life insurance is better than too little for the survivors.

The next question after determining how much life insurance is needed is: What type of life insurance and how much does it cost? There is always a budget question involved and the cost will depend on which type of insurance you choose. To simplify we will review 4 types:

1. **Term**: lowest cost but has no cash value; only a death benefit

2. **Whole Life:** oldest type; is more expensive and has cash value build up, tax free, inside the plan; not very flexible

3. **Universal Life:** similar to whole life; more expensive with cash value build up, but more flexible with adjustable premiums and death benefits

4. **Variable Life:** usually in a universal life package with flexible premiums but cash value is "invested" and adjusted at will, in sub-accounts similar to mutual funds.

Some bottom line issues make the choices more clear. For example, if you are younger and have a limited budget, Term is the best choice because it's inexpensive. Since life insurance is based on age, Term for people as they age can get quite expensive. This cost can be mitigated however, by purchasing a 25 year level premium term policy, for example, at age 50, so you are covered until age 75, instead of paying higher premiums each year.

If your goal is cash value, tax-free growth with the idea you may someday tap into the cash value, then a Universal or Variable policy may be a better choice. If the goal is permanent insurance for life, term is not a good fit because the word "term" implies a length of time. Term insurance ends after a certain term, but the policy may allow you to convert to permanent insurance before the policy ends. For example, this conversion option is important because it allows a person who owns a 15 year term policy to convert before the 10th year. Suppose the person contracted diabetes in year 9 and would likely struggle to get the insurance renewed unless the premium was rated up because of the disease. The conversion allows the person to receive permanent insurance for life without evidence of insurability. The premiums will be higher, but it may be worth the price.

Life insurance can be complicated and there are many reasons to own life insurance. Estate planning often uses life insurance as a protection against estate taxes or as a way to replace a charitable gift to a trust, so the children can inherit money. Sometimes mortgage companies and car loan companies sell term insurance to pay off the loan in case of death. (We recommend not doing this through the loan company because the premium often times is more expensive than traditional term insurance.)

We highly recommend a check-up on your life insurance every couple of years. Life changes constantly and risk changes as well. In our many meetings with clients, we see the same problems with life insurance over and over. These problems can be critical and must be addressed. Most people do not have enough insurance, while other have insurance that costs too much or does not meet their financial goals. Older clients have outdated policies or too much cash value building up with too little death benefit. A critical point to remember is that the moment a death occurs; it is too late to fix a problem. You are a candidate for a life insurance check up!

Notes

"An investment in knowledge always
pays the best interest."
(Benjamin Franklin)

"If you think education is expensive, try ignorance."
Derek Bok

Chapter 14

Education Plans For Kids: Do They Really Ever Leave Home?

Every parent aspires for their children to go to college. Every grandparent aspires for their grandchildren to attend "the university." And why not? Statistics validate the fact that the higher a person rises into the education system, the higher potential income that person receives during their lifetime. Education is often measured in terms of income potential, but it is really about increasing the opportunities for someone and providing a broad base of intellectual framework in which to build a better life. A common question is, "How can we afford to provide such educational opportunities?"

This is a valid question because higher education is a costly venture. Public universities today can cost $40,000 to $60,000 for a four year degree while private colleges are costing $60,000 to $120,000. If you add graduate school, medical school or law school, the cost can become too much for the mind to comfortably absorb. A second troubling factor, besides the outright cost, is the inflation rate attached to the costs. For decades the annual inflation rate for college expenses has been much higher than the inflation rate for the economy. It seems to be a rule of thumb that if the economic inflation rate is 2-3% annually, inflation rate on education is 5-7% annually. Clearly a parent or grandparent who starts financial planning for education in the early years of a child's life will have a distinct advantage over one who starts late in the game.

I once had a client, during the process of listing their financial goals, who said, "I need a college fund for my daughter." Of course I heartily agreed and asked the following question: "How old is your child?"

The mother looked at me square in the eyes and said, "She's finishing up the 10th grade."

I looked back and replied half jokingly, but half seriously, "Pray for a scholarship!"

One of my favorite quotes about investing came from the lips of Albert Einstein, when asked, "What is the greatest discovery of mankind?" He thought for a second and said, "Compound interest!" His answer is the perfect solution for a college savings plan.

The earlier one starts to save and invest, the more the assets build up and the less money has to be invested overall.

The first principle to creating a college education plan is to start early in the child's life. The second principle is to save and fund the plan regularly. This brings us to the third principle, choosing the best vehicle to accomplish the goal.

There are at least three vehicles available today that are very appropriate for education planning. These are not the only three. After all, many parents have borrowed from their 401(K) plan or used home equity loans to help put their kids through college. Parents and grandparents often sacrifice greatly to give their young loved ones a chance in life. However, three strategies work particularly well because they are designed with education in mind. Not only that, but they have interesting tax incentives as well. And anything that saves taxes is worth investigating.

The first and oldest of these plans is the custodial account under the acronyms UGMA or UTMA accounts (Uniform Gift or Trust to Minors Act). These accounts are easy to set up and usually cost no more to set up than a regular investment account. The idea is simple. A parent or grandparent sets up the account with a mutual fund, brokerage firm or bank. The adult is the custodian of the account but the account is set up using the child's social security number. This account is given tax incentives by the IRS. Until the child turns 14 years old, the first $750 per year of investment earnings is tax exempt. For example, a $5,000 account with a 10% return this year ($500) is tax-free. The next $750 earnings above the $750 per year are taxed in the child's tax bracket. After age 14, the taxes on earnings are charged to the child's tax bracket, but usually teenagers do not earn much money and the taxes therefore, should be minimal.

Like all investment strategies, there are risks as well as rewards. The major risk of the custodial account is not the investment risk which of course is inherent in every strategy, but is related to the child's age. Every custodial account asset, if not used, will become the property of the child when age 18 or 21, depending on which state you are residing. Think about it carefully; this could become a potential problem. I once had a client with over $100,000 in their kid's custodial account. They had faithfully invested for their children and should be commended. But what if the child went off on the wild side, got into drugs or something even worse? Technically, unless the parents spent the money for the child before age 21 in North Carolina, that child could cash out the account and run with the money. This event could turn into a disaster.

Caution is the proper word in this instance. First, I remind parents that they do not have to tell their children about the custodial account as the child is growing up. Let it be a surprise. Secondly, the custodial account, unlike the next two strategies we will review, does not have to be earmarked for educational expenses. For instance, a parent could help the child purchase their first car with custodial money, or buy a prom dress for their daughter. There are few restrictions as long as the money is spent on the child, not the adult. This expenditure is based on the honor system, but pity the parent who goes through an audit by the IRS and cannot document where the custodial money was spent.

There is a second helpful vehicle for education planning and that is the Coverdell IRA, formerly called the Education IRA. Today one can set up a Coverdell IRA with a maximum contribution of $2,000 per year per child or with as little as $25.00/month. As a matter of fact some parents prefer the monthly bank draft method of $50 or $100 per month into an education plan account. As in the custodial account, the Coverdell IRA can be set up with a mutual fund, brokerage account or bank. This IRA is restricted to educational expenses regardless of the child's age.

The tax incentive is significant. All earnings inside the Coverdell IRA grow tax deferred and are not taxed upon withdrawal as long as it is used for education expenses. Clearly if this account was set up for a young child and funded every year at $2,000, and invested properly, the tax benefits would be significant.

One disadvantage of the Coverdell IRA is the limit of a $2,000 per year contribution. The other education plans allow more, up to $11,000 annually under current law (the annual contribution or gift is regulated by the IRS gift rule limitation of $11,000 per year per person tax free gift). A second disadvantage is that if there is money left in the IRA when the child or beneficiary turns 30 years of age, the IRA must be closed down and a 10% tax paid on the earnings left in the account.

A third popular education plan is called the 529 Plan. These plans are technically under the fiduciary responsibility of the 50 states, so all 529 Plans are tied to one of the states. However, regardless of which state the 529 Plan is attached or what state your child plans to go to college or your state of residence, all plans are available to you.

A helpful benefit of the 529 Plan is its flexibility, one being the choice of beneficiary. Any person in the immediate family, including nieces, nephews and even cousins, can be the beneficiary on the plan. Even more interesting, the beneficiary can be changed at will at any time. This means that one single 529 Plan can suffice for the whole family. Let's say that you have two children three years apart. When the older one becomes a college senior, you can withdraw money from the 529 Plan for the semester's tuition. The next day you can change the beneficiary for child number two and withdraw their tuition for the freshman year. The plan is so flexible that you, the parent, can go back to community college for a refresher course and pull money out for yourself. Simply call in and make yourself the plan beneficiary for that particular withdrawal.

Like the Coverdell IRA, 529 Plan assets grow tax deferred and are tax free if used for higher education expenses. Here-in lays a weakness in the 529 Plan. Notice we said "higher education expenses." Money cannot be used from a 529 Plan (with tax benefits) for pre-college level education expenses, but only for accredited college expenses. The good news is that there are several accredited golf and culinary colleges out there in case you needed a refresher course!

Gifts or contributions to 529 Plans are limited to $11,000 annually, but there is a special caveat. The caveat is especially important for estate tax purposes. A person, say, a wealthy grandparent, can contribute as much as a $55,000 one-time gift to a grandchild or child. The gift goes out of the estate. After five years, the $55,000 (which equals $11,000 x 5 years) is permanently out of the estate and therefore not subject to estate taxes. Two wealthy grandparents could theoretically gift $55,000 each to all six of their grandchildren and in effect remove $660,000 ($110,000 x 6) out of their estate. Not only is this a good tax strategy, but also the grandparents can be comforted by the fact that the money has to be used for educating the grandkids through college.

Unlike the other two plans which have age restrictions on the child, the 529 Plan does not. If a parent had two children go to college but still had $20,000 left in the 529 Plan, they could let it grow tax free for their grandkids, or help educate their nieces and nephews. Better yet, they could keep it until they were retired, take advantage of the years of tax deferred growth and then pull the money out during their retirement years and pay only a 10% penalty plus tax on their earnings.

Education planning can be enjoyable and exciting. Knowing that a little child will grow up with the potential of reaching that milestone of a college degree is extremely rewarding.

Creating a proper strategy when the child is young will enhance the likelihood of a dream being fulfilled.

Notes

_____

_____

_____

_____

_____

_____

_____

_____

_____

_____

_____

_____

"All prosperity begins in the mind and is dependent only on the full use of our creative imagination."
(Ruth Ross)

"All the breaks you need in life wait within your imagination. Imagination is the workshop of your mind, capable of turning mind energy into accomplishment and wealth."
Napoleon Hill

Chapter 15

New Years Resolutions: The Top 10 Plus 1

As each New Year approaches, many people evaluate the past year and often times are not satisfied with the way their lives are going. What they tend to focus on is what is visible – things such as diet, exercise, etc. I believe that many avoid making resolutions concerning their financial picture because they don't know which part of it to tackle first. As I see it, there are potentially eleven areas you should tackle. While that might seem formidable, don't let it paralyze you from getting started. Procrastination not only costs time but money as well. You can choose from the eleven I have listed in the order of their importance in your life. Each change you make has an impact on the other ten areas because some of these are inter-related.

Let me cover these resolutions one at a time.

1 Pay yourself first.

Many times this is a resolution that is easier said than done. You must first analyze your budget, get a grip on the spending and expenses, be honest about the income and then make a promise to pay yourself first. Treat yourself as a creditor, a bill you must pay. You can commit as much as 10% of your net check or a certain dollar amount such as $25.00 or $50.00 every paycheck. Do this by automatic withdrawal from your checking account every time a paycheck goes in and soon this becomes a habit, a good habit! This will become your personal/emergency fund. As it builds, your reliance on credit cards for emergencies will drop dramatically. After your emergency fund reaches three to six months of your expenses, then the money could be directed towards other investments or goals. Living on 90% of your income is not as difficult as you imagine!

2 Fund your retirement plans.

It has always puzzled me why people would not want to take advantage of the biggest wealth accumulation vehicle of our time—Company 401K's or company retirement plans. No taxes are paid on the money contributed or on the interest, dividends or capital gains earned until they are withdrawn. When your employer is contributing to your retirement plan or matching your contribution, that money is "free money"... take it! You can only take advantage of this by contributing yourself on a matching plan. You may feel as if this will put a strain on your budget, but remember

158

as I said before; no taxes are paid on this contribution. For example, if your income is $500/week and your contribution is $50/week, then you pay taxes only on $450.

Oftentimes the investment options in a 401K, 403(b) or Simple IRA are mutual funds. Many of us have experienced volatility in our mutual funds and stocks, but remember 401K investing employs a concept known as dollar cost averaging (DCA). What this means is consistently, systematically investing a certain amount every month. Your employer deducts money out of your paycheck every month and forwards it to your retirement plan. What does this mean for you?

Month	Amt. Invested	Price/Share	# of Shares Purchased of Mutual Fund
1	$100.00	$10.00	10
2	$100.00	$5.00	20

Notice something; when the price per share was $10.00, you purchased 10 shares with your $100.00, but the next month the mutual fund dropped in value so you were able to purchase more shares with the same amount of money. You are buying fewer shares at higher prices and more shares at lower prices over time. Now your average cost per share is $200 / 30 shares = $6.67/share, so even if the share price goes up to only $7.00/share, you have made money.

Remember it's not timing the market but time in the market. If you stick to consistent investing over time, you will be rewarded.

3 Review life insurance, health insurance, disability, casualty and long term care (LTC).

> **Life Insurance:** There are 2 kinds of life insurance – temporary and permanent. Term insurance covers you for a specific term, i.e.; coverage for 10, 15 or 20 years (yes, there are 20 year term policies) to cover your life while kids are growing up or until you are debt free. It is best to secure level term in lieu of increasing term. Level term requires payments to remain the same during the term of your policy. Not all term insurance policies are good. For example, a poor choice of term insurance is mortgage insurance, for your home mortgage payoff incase you die. Be careful because it is more expensive than level term policies. It is important to remember here that once the term is up you have no insurance coverage. Many people choose term due to premiums being more affordable. For example, in my situation, I am married with 2 children, one entering college and the other entering middle school. My husband and I chose to do a 20 year term for additional coverage to cover our lives while they were in school. We each received $500,000 of coverage and the monthly premium for both was $112.00 (46 year old female and 46 year old male), considerably less expensive than permanent insurance.
>
> Permanent life insurance is available in three varieties: variable, whole life and universal life. Whole life covers you for your entire life; fixed premiums, guaranteed never to go up. In addition,

whole life builds cash value, tax deferred. The company invests this cash value in fixed investment instruments usually yielding a guaranteed rate of 4% to 5%.

Variable life insurance allows the investing of cash value into sub-accounts which are like mutual funds, thus no guarantees. If the fund goes down in value, so does your cash value. What is the risk? You are right if you said your policy could be cancelled due to lack of funds (built up cash value) someday in the future. Unless you are one that is able to "over fund" the cash value (putting in more than the required premium) or the sub-accounts grow strongly over the years, then another type of insurance may be best for you.

Universal life insurance has cash value as well, but is only growing with an interest rate that adjusts annually (no funds or sub-accounts). Keep in mind that if the interest rate assumption used by the carrier (life insurance company) is wrong, the policy will not perform as planned. This could mean increasing premiums in later years or even a lapsed policy. However, if the interest rates are better than assumed, your premiums could decrease.

Now here is the question: "Which type is better?"And to that I have to respond, "It depends."

If you want to have certainty that your premiums never increase, then whole life or a guaranteed level premium term life should be your choice. If you are comfortable with the possibility that your premiums could change (increase or decrease) in the future, then universal life or variable life insurance is the answer. If you have no problem "over funding" (putting in additional money) your policy and want potential gains that match the stock market, then variable life would be the answer.

My advice is to buy insurance for exactly what it is – insuring against loss. Don't try to insure for investment purposes. It is also good to analyze your insurance needs at least every 2 years just to make sure you are adequately covered.

➢ **Health Insurance:** We have a health care crisis in our country today. There are fewer corporations offering health insurance as a benefit to retirees, so many people delay retirement until 65 in order to move from private insurance to Medicare. Often times those who face layoffs are also faced with losing insurance coverage. After leaving a company plan, Cobra insurance is available for an 18-month period. But unless employment is secured by the end of the 18-month period, what do you do? There are insurance companies that provide temporary, short-term coverage. You can also hold down the cost by choosing higher deductibles.

➢ **Disability Insurance:** Many of us feel that our biggest asset is our home or retirement plan, but actually it is the ability to earn an income. Statistics show that the likelihood of a disability is greater than the likelihood of death before retirement years. Life's savings can be lost due to disability. Disability insurance can seem expensive but again, losing everything could be more expensive! Also the longer the waiting period you have before collecting benefits (60 days, 180 days, etc.), the lower the cost of coverage. Meet with your financial planner and work out a program that fits your needs and budget. You can't afford not to protect your earnings potential.

➢ **Casualty Insurance:** Anyone owning property knows the value of insuring your car and home. A good analysis of your policy with a reputable agent is a must. Sit down with him or her and evaluate what you are trying to protect and then make sure you have proper coverage. Remember to include inflation protection on your homeowner's policy.

➢ **Long Term Care Insurance (LTC):** Many years ago families lived in close proximity to each other and someone was at home during the day, so caring for the elder parent or grandparent was no big deal. Today families have both parents working and they don't live within the same area any longer, so the need for extended care is much greater than in the past.

The fact is two out of every five Americans will enter a nursing home at some point in their lives. Many believe that Medicaid, a tax funded public assistance program, will not withstand the demographic tidal wave of aging baby boomers. According to the census, the fastest growing age group in our country is those over 85 years of age. People are living longer due to knowledge of how to take better care of themselves and improved health care. The longer we live the more our bodies just wear out. It's not unusual that as we age, we could potentially have up to five chronic illnesses to contend with.

After age 50, Long Term Care Insurance needs
to be added to one's list of protection strategies.

4 Review your debts and strategies to pay off debt.

None of us enjoy being in debt, so how do we get out
and stay out? The first place to begin is to analyze all of
your debt. Create columns on a sheet of paper and list each
debt owed. In the second column, list the amount owed to
each, and next, list the interest rate you are charged on the
debt. Now carefully look at the interest rate of each. Focus
on the debts with the highest rate. Commit to pay more than
the minimum payment each time on the debts with the highest rate. Continue to pay aggressively until each creditor is
eliminated, and then focus on the next debt that has the
highest interest rate. Keep repeating this process until all
creditors are eliminated even if it takes a long time.

Another strategy is to secure a consolidated loan at a
lower rate. If you chose this strategy, stick to the payments
and do not go into debt again. Be careful because some loan
companies charge high interest rates with little flexibility of
payments.

Mortgages do not fall into the category of "pay off
early". Usually, mortgages are "good debt" and you can
deduct the interest, saving taxes. So if you are making extra
payments on your mortgage, **stop**, and apply that to credit
cards or consumer debt. See a financial planner and let them
help you structure a debt reduction plan. Get out of debt as
soon as possible! Do it now!

5 Evaluate budget and cash flow.

One of the most difficult exercises to do is to keep a log of everything on which you spend money. I don't mean just the big items, but all the little ones too. I challenge you to keep a log on everything you buy. For example, keep track of every purchase of soft drink, coffee, lunch, dinner, etc. for 30 days. You will be amazed at the outcome. I have met with clients where the result after 30 days ranged anywhere from $400 to $800 per month just in lunches, soft drinks, snacks and dinners, especially eating out. I did this for my own family and yes; I was guilty of a whopping $800 per month in lunches, dinners, etc. Needless to say, I felt sick that I, as a financial planner, could be so wasteful. I immediately made changes. My children experienced culture shock because no longer were there fast runs through the drive-thru. I began planning quicker meals to prepare at home like spaghetti, soups and sandwiches.

The food budget is only one area where money could be wasted. Every budget item is a "candidate" to cut down to size in order to live within your means. You must get a handle on this early while there is time to make adjustments. You may want to use our budget and cash flow worksheet (See Chapter 3).

6 Create education plans for kids and grandkids.

It is very difficult to qualify for government loans and grants, so even starting a small monthly contribution is wise when the children are young. There are several ways to prepare and plan for future college expenses.

➤ **529 Plan:** A friendly, consumer oriented college savings plan that grows tax deferred and when used for college expenses can be withdrawn tax free.

➤ **UGMA:** Uniform Gift to Minors Act. Under this plan, the assets, managed by the adult, belong to the child and the law requires that the assets be used for the benefit of the child. Money in a UGMA can be used for almost anything that is for the benefit and welfare of the child. Assets in a UGMA account belong to the child at age 18. Many find UGMA accounts to be beneficial because taxes are much lower on the earnings and this account does not limit the parent to just college expenses.

➤ **UTMA:** Uniform Transfer to Minors Act. The UTMA offers the same benefits as the UGMA with the exception that asset transfer can be delayed until age 21.

➤ **Coverdell IRA:** Up to $2,000 per year of contributions are allowed into the IRA. Assets grow tax deferred and can be withdrawn tax free for school expenses at any age.

➤ **College Prepayment Plans:** Stay away from these plans! This plan allows you to send in a certain amount of money now and in turn, you are guaranteed your child's college tuition will be covered. The problems with this are:

   ◆ These programs cover tuition only. Room and board makes up a good 40-60% of the cost of college.

   ◆ No guarantee your child will be accepted to the school or that he/she will want to attend the school after high school.

   ◆ There are tax liabilities (consult a tax advisor).

7 Refinance Mortgage.

It is always wise to stay on top of current interest rates. Even a 1% difference in rates can save money. You can refinance by calling your current mortgage holder and inquiring about reducing your rate through what is called a "stream line mortgage". The market is very competitive and your mortgage company does not want to lose your business, so stand firm in your rights to secure a lower interest rate if possible. If "stream line" refinancing is not available, then "shop around" with other mortgage lenders for better rates. Over the life of the mortgage, thousands of dollars may be saved.

8 Review Income Tax Exemptions and Deductions.

If you receive a sizable tax refund each year, you should consult with your accountant and payroll department to increase exemptions and lower your tax withholding. This clearly will increase your cash flow. Do not allow the government to become your savings account. Remember to change tax exemptions when you get married, buy a primary residence or a second home or have a child.

9 Review your Giving Strategies.

Think of all the good you will be able to do with all the money you now have from doing just eight of the resolutions. Giving back can make your community and thus your world a better place. It is difficult to explain the feeling of personal gratification from giving and what it does. Think about the times you sit down to pay bills; it takes some joy out of your day. Now think about the times you have written a check to your church or favorite charity or when you bought a present for a child for the Angel Tree Ministry. What a different feeling! It puts the skip back in your step and a warm feeling in your heart. Giving really helps the giver more than the recipient. Ten percent of your income would be a nice goal to start but give what you can. Tax deductions are allowed for giving to church or charity.

10 Evaluate the Quality of your Financial Advice.

Financial advice is only as good as the person giving it. If you meet with an advisor and right away they push you as to where to invest your money – run and run fast! True financial planners take time to get to know you. They ask questions and take notes; they want to know your goals for the short term as well as those in the future. What is recommended to you must make sense financially. Trust your instinct and ask questions. Get more than one opinion on your plan. Ask yourself, "Does this person have my best interest at heart?" Then ask them, "How will you make money?" This will reveal the intent and integrity of the advice. A quality advisor is invaluable to your financial future.

11 Review your Wills and Estate Plan.

Everyone has an estate. It is important to have a will and a plan for your estate. This lets everyone know how and to whom you want your assets to transfer after your death. You should review your will every 3-5 years because situations in families can change. I have met with a number of clients over the years that were victims of an outdated will. One of my clients who I will call Jane was born in 1964 to a doctor. I make the point of letting you know that her father was a doctor because by being a professional, one would believe that he was well versed in knowing the importance of a will being current. Jane's father passed away with a will that was dated 1961, three years *prior* to Jane's birth. The problem was that at her father's death, Jane's brother inherited everything because Jane's mom had already passed on. Jane's brother had a gambling habit and had served time in prison. She came to me for advice, desperate for help, but it was too late!

Sometimes divorced couples fail to update their wills and the old wills leaves everything to the divorced ex-spouse. This becomes a real problem in the case of marrying again. Obviously the new spouse would not be very happy if the old spouse is the recipient of the assets or if the grown children from the previous marriage are the sole beneficiaries.

There are many clients that I meet who have never completed a will. What a mistake! The court then decides who distributes your assets and who gets custody of your children. Trusts can be another important tool for an estate plan and also need to be reviewed. I have seen cases where a trust was set up to handle a certain need or to help distribute assets in a particular way and the verbiage in the trust was not correct. What a mistake! It is too late, once the person who created the trust dies.

An example of this happened with a senior client I'll call Joe. Joe had done a careful job of setting up his will, creating a trust to care for his special needs daughter. He thought he had created a trust to protect his daughter from losing all of her assets to long term care. She was going to need care for the rest of her life (care he had always given to her would have to be done by professionals after his death). Upon review of the trust, I discovered that he did not set up the trust correctly to accomplish his wishes. I recommended that he meet with a different attorney from the one who set up the initial trust, and the new attorney validated that he needed to correct the trust document. He was so grateful that a simple review and second opinion had finally created a way for his special needs daughter to have income that would go directly to her and not harm the qualification to receive other aid.

The two points I am trying to make to you are to review your wills, trusts and estate plans to ensure they remain current. Also, get a second opinion.

These New Year's resolutions should be on your "to-do" list each year. Just like an annual physical received by your doctor, a financial check-up is needed for your financial well being. Then your future will be one of security and stability. Be diligent; be courageous!

Notes

_____

_____

_____

_____

_____

_____

_____

_____

_____

_____

_____

_____

About the Authors

Greg Hicks, CFP graduated from NC State University, 1968, with a BS in Chemical Engineering, and from International Christian Graduate University, 1979, with a Masters of Religion degree.

His athletic career includes winning two Atlantic Coast Conference championships in the sport of Wrestling. After college, he competed for the United States as a wrestler for Athletes in Action, in the 82 kg. (180.5 lbs.) weight class at the 1973 and 1974 World Championships in Istanbul, Turkey, and Minsk, Russia, respectively. In 1975, he won the Gold Medal in Mexico City, representing the USA in the Pan American Games, and was a silver medalist in the World Cup Tournament.

In 1981, after serving as assistant national director of Athletes in Action, a division of Campus Crusade for Christ, he became general manager of the Memphis Americans, a professional soccer team in Memphis, TN.

In 1985, he became a financial planner and investment advisor, and in 1990 became a Certified Financial Planner. In 1987, he started his own business called *Financial Resource Management, Inc.* The business has since expanded to include six employees, with offices in three North Carolina cities. He and his staff provide advisory services to almost 1,000 clients, spread across 15 different states.

He hosts two weekly radio shows in Raleigh, NC and Morehead City, NC, and sponsors several seminars yearly across North Carolina, all under the banner, "The Financial Fair." He is also a popular teacher and speaker in various settings across North Carolina.

Greg is the co-author of the book, *The Truth About Lies: Navigating the Dangers of Deception.* He is active in Crossroads Fellowship Church, and resides in Raleigh, NC with his wife, Sue. He has two children, Cari and Nathan, and a son-in-law, Eric.

Wanda Cooper, CSA joined Financial Resource Management, Inc. in March of 1997 after working in the banking industry for 18 years. Wanda managed two branches of First Union National Bank in Raleigh, NC and specialized in small business and mortgage lending. She received her Series 6 and 63 Licenses in 1992 while with the bank and began personal investment counseling. She received her NC Life and Health Insurance License in 1995, her Medicare Supplement and Long Term Care Insurance License in 1997 and her Series 7 in 1999 and became a Certified Senior Advisor in 2003.

Wanda is active in the Clayton community and is an active member of Mount Moriah Baptist Church. She is married and lives in Clayton with her husband, Rick, and their two children, Richard and Jordan.

*You may order books, or request
information about scheduling
Greg Hicks or Wanda Cooper
for speaking engagements, by calling
Financial Resource Management, Inc.
at 800-487-1786 or by logging on
http://www.financialfair.com.*

*Books are also available at selected
bookstores and can be ordered
through http://www.amazon.com.*